ACCIDENTS

In North American Climbing 2021

Volume 12 | Number 2 | Issue 74

AMERICAN ALPINE CLUB
GOLDEN, COLORADO

ALPINE CLUB OF CANADA
CANMORE, ALBERTA

CONTENTS

8   **Preface**

FEATURE ARTICLES

10   **Know the Ropes: Cleaning Sport Climbs**

ACCIDENTS & ANALYSIS

20   **USA**
110   **Canada**
122   **Mexico**
123   **Backcountry Avalanches**

ESSENTIALS

37   **Wilderness Medicine**
41   **Climbing and Heat Illness**
59   **Dynamic Belaying: The Soft Catch**

DATA TABLES

138   **Tables**

Front Cover: Dalton Bunker climbing in the Wicked Cave, Rifle, CO. Photo by Tara Kerzhner.
Back Cover: Avalanche near Ophir, CO. See page 123 for a new section of avalanche reports and analysis. Photo courtesy of Colorado Avalanche Information Center.

© **2021 The American Alpine Club**

ISBN: 978-1-7356956-4-8; (e-book) 978-1-7356956-5-5. Manufactured in the United States. Published by the American Alpine Club, 710 Tenth Street, Suite 100, Golden, CO, 80401.

WARNING!
The activities described within Accidents in North American Climbing (ANAC)—including but not limited to: rock climbing, ice climbing, mountaineering, backcountry skiing, or any other outdoor activity—carry a significant risk of personal injury or death. The owners, staff, contributors, and volunteers that create this publication recommend that you DO NOT participate in these activities unless you are an expert, have sought or obtained qualified professional instruction or guidance, are knowledgeable about the risks involved, and are willing to assume personal responsibility for all the risks associated with these activities. ANAC and its publisher, the American Alpine Club, MAKE NO WARRANTIES, EXPRESSED OR IMPLIED, OF ANY KIND REGARDING THE CONTENTS OF THIS PUBLICATION, AND EXPRESSLY DISCLAIM ANY WARRANTY REGARDING THE ACCURACY OR RELIABILITY OF INFORMATION CONTAINED HEREIN. The American Alpine Club further disclaims any responsibility for injuries or death incurred by any person engaging in these activities. Use the information contained in this publication at your own risk, and do not depend on the information contained herein for personal safety or for determining whether to attempt any climb, route, or activity described herein. The examples/stories contained herein are anecdotal and/or informational only and are not intended to represent advice, recommendations, or commentary on appropriate conduct, standards or choices that you, the reader, may make regarding your own activities.

ACCIDENTS IN NORTH AMERICAN CLIMBING

Volume 12 | Number 2 | Issue 74

American Alpine Club

EDITOR EMERITUS
John E. (Jed) Williamson

EDITOR
Dougald MacDonald

DESIGN
David Boersma – Mojave Creative Lab

CONTRIBUTING EDITORS
Aram Attarian (NC), Dave Weber (AK)

REGIONAL EDITORS
Daniel Apodaca (NM and AZ); Lindsay Auble (KY and TN); Mark Berenblum (Upstate NY); Dan Cousins (New England); Stefani Dawn (NV); Ashton Johnston and Bill Kinter (CO); Michelle Leber and Sarah Wolfe (UT); Michael Habicht, Lauren DeLaunay Miller, and Christy Rosa Mohler (CA); Stacia Glenn (WA); Molly Herber (WY); Gary O'Brien (ID and MT); Eric Ratkowski (Shawangunks, NY); Michael Wejchert (NH)

ADDITIONAL THANKS
adidas Outdoor, Lindsay Auble, Austin BeckDoss, Christine Blackmon, Coros, Elizabeth Cromwell, Desert Mountain Medicine, Tara Kerzhner, Melissa Lester, Hilaree Nelson, Leo Paik, Jim Pasterczyk, Adam Peters, Ian Jackson, R. Bryan Simon

Alpine Club of Canada

CANADA EDITOR
Robert Chisnall
anam@alpineclubofcanada.ca

Built for Adventure

The COROS VERTIX GPS Watch navigation features are powered by 60 hours of full accuracy GPS battery to keep you moving forward on your next adventure.

PREFACE

By Dougald MacDonald

Last year was a strange one for climbers, to say the least. COVID-19 seems to have brought far more climbers to some areas—with an increase in accidents—while other areas had unusually low numbers, primarily because of long COVID-related closures. (We had no reports at all from Denali National Park, for example.) On balance, the number of incidents and fatalities was down in 2020 compared with recent years.

We've introduced three new items this year. First, with the support of adidas Outdoors, we have translated the 2020 edition of ANAC into Spanish. This project is intended to increase access to our work in North America (especially Mexico) and throughout the Spanish-speaking world. The effort was led by Mexican climber Omar Gaytán, with help from a crew of Mexican and U.S. volunteers. The PDF of *Accidentes de Escalada en Norteamérica* can be downloaded for free at the AAC website.

We've also updated our annual data tables with some new categories, tracking accidents by climbing style and "rope position" (leading, top-roping, rappelling, etc.). We've updated some accident causes to better reflect modern climbing and archived others. (The archived tables are at *publications.americanalpineclub.org.*) Colorado climber Bill Kinter worked hard to make these revisions possible.

Our biggest addition is a new section on backcountry skiing and snowboarding avalanches. This publication has always covered avalanches, but not backcountry touring. Now we're reporting on a selection of incidents from the latest winter season, drawing on the incredible analyses published by various U.S. avalanche centers. Professional skier Hilaree Nelson, a member of the AAC board of directors, inspired this project, which was assisted by ANAC team members Michelle Leber and Gary O'Brien. Let us know what you think: *accidents@americanalpineclub.org.*

Most avalanche centers use similar language in reports about fatalities, such as this paragraph from the Shasta Avalanche Center: "Fatal avalanche accidents are tragic events. We describe them to help people involved and the community as a whole to better understand them. We offer these comments in hope that they will help people avoid future avalanche accidents and offer our condolences to family, friends, and others affected by this unfortunate event." The same spirit of knowledge building and information sharing, tempered with sensitivity to the anguish suffered in our community after any accident, steers all of our work at this publication.

Submissions
Share your story and help fellow climbers! Visit *publications.americanalpineclub.org* to file an accident report online. Or email us at *accidents@americanalpineclub.org.*

Friends of Accidents in North American Climbing
The following people donated $100 or more in 2020 specifically to support *Accidents.* Thank you! Make your own contribution at *americanalpineclub.org/donate.*

Jim Austin	Yannick Gingras	John & Rebecca Soebbing
Laura Chedalawada	Eric Green	Kevin Smith
Charlie Eiriksson	Kurt Lustgarten	Doug Wilson
Carla Firey	Dougald MacDonald	Sara & Owen Zacharias
Clark Gerhardt	Benjamin Malave	

Protect yourself.

Climbing can be a risky pursuit, but one worth the price of admission. With the newly enhanced Emergency Rescue & Medical Expense coverage of Membership 2.0, you can tie in a little easier knowing the American Alpine Club is on belay. No matter where you are in the world, if disaster strikes, we'll rescue you from the crag, get you to the hospital, and even help pay your deductible or other direct medical expenses once you're there.

With enhanced rescue and medical expense coverage, national policy initiatives, publications such as the *Accidents in North American Climbing*, discounts, lodging, and more, the AAC has supported climbers for over 120 years. Learn more about the Club and join at americanalpineclub.org/join.

You belong here.

Tramming in to the next draw while cleaning a steep route at the Red River Gorge. This technique helps the climber get back to the wall and lessens the swing after each draw is cleaned. *Johnny Nowell*

Know the Ropes

CLEANING SPORT ROUTES

Efficient methods for cleaning overhanging climbs

BY LINDSAY AUBLE

Y ou've trained for months to send a classic overhanging sport climb. You've spent day after day in the gym, improving your power and endurance. You must have watched dozens of YouTube videos, dialing in that beta. When the day arrives, you crush the route first go while hanging the draws. An Ondra-level flash. The crowd goes wild.

But wait...now you have to clean the route. At least the anchors are similar to those in the gym, with carabiners on the chains where you can clip your rope. As you lower, you start to kick out, creating momentum so you can reach your next draw. It's hard! It ends up taking you three times as long to clean as it did to climb. At the bottom, you drag your belayer off a boulder, through a bush, and into a tree. Yikes.

At the Red River Gorge, my home crag, we often see strong climbers waltz up an overhanging route only to fumble the cleaning process. It doesn't have to be that way. This article will help you safely and efficiently clean your draws after leading a steep single-pitch climb. The techniques described here apply to bolted or mostly bolted routes, though they also can be used to clean single-pitch traditionally protected climbs. These techniques become particularly useful on overhanging and traversing routes—any climb where the bolt line is not directly under the anchors and the cleaning climber will take large swings when retrieving gear.

AT THE ANCHORS

Until your party is done with a route, the anchor should be equipped with your own gear for lowering or top-roping. Do this even if there are drop-in lowering hooks (a.k.a. mussy hooks) or fixed carabiners at the anchors. Lowering or top-roping from your own equipment saves wear and tear on the permanent anchor—which is a community resource.

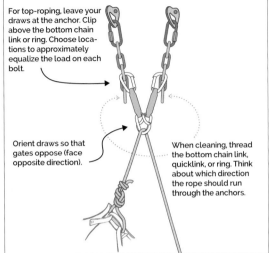

For top-roping, leave your draws at the anchor. Clip above the bottom chain link or ring. Choose locations to approximately equalize the load on each bolt.

Orient draws so that gates oppose (face opposite direction).

When cleaning, thread the bottom chain link, quicklink, or ring. Think about which direction the rope should run through the anchors.

To equip the anchor with quickdraws for lowering or a TR:

- Clip at least two draws or slings to the anchor. Orient your draws so they are opposed and approximately equalized.
- A locker draw (a quickdraw with locking carabiners on each end) will increase the security of a top-rope anchor.
- If possible, do not clip your draws to the bottom chain link, quicklink, ring, etc., on the anchor. This makes it easier for the final climber to clean the anchor.
- Avoid quickdraw placements that would cause the carabiners to be weight-loaded over an edge.
- A draw with a steel carabiner on the rope side will last much longer for frequent top-

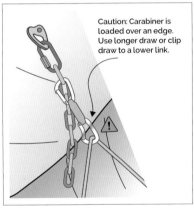

Caution: Carabiner is loaded over an edge. Use longer draw or clip draw to a lower link.

roping. (The Edelrid Bulletproof, an aluminum carabiner with a wear-resistant steel insert in the basket, comes in locking and non-locking options.) As a bonus, steel at the anchors reduces grime on your rope.

Once everyone is done with a climb, it's time to clean your gear from the anchor and the route. Before the cleaning climber leaves the ground, make a plan. The climber and belayer should discuss what cleaning method will be used (lower or rappel) and the steps involved. They should also discuss what verbal (or non-verbal) cues will be used and what they mean. This is especially important when communication is difficult between the anchor and belay locations.

For cleaning the gear from really steep climbs, assuming no one is seconding the route, it is generally safest and easiest to do it while lowering. At today's busy sport crags, with active local climbing organizations (LCOs) and modern anchor systems, lowering has become widely accepted—even recommended—at many areas. (A few climbers and local organizations still recommend rappelling to clean—learn more about the local cleaning ethic through guidebooks, Mountain Project, the LCO's social media or website, or by visiting the local climbing gym/outfitter.) If rappelling from an anchor is necessary because it's the local ethic, the anchor hardware is worn, or it's a remote climb where anchors are rarely maintained, it's often easiest to follow the route on top-rope and *then* rappel, rather than trying to clean on rappel. Always incorporate a backup, and be sure your rope ends are knotted.

CLEANING THE ANCHORS

If you are reading this article to learn how to clean steep routes, you probably already know how to thread the rope through the anchors and prepare for lowering or rappelling. If not, there are plenty of resources available to learn this skill, including videos produced by the AAC and AMGA. If you haven't cleaned a route before, it is imperative to practice in a safe environment with feedback from an experienced climber. It is becoming more common to see practice anchors at popular crags. Ask your local climbing gym if they have or can set up practice anchors. Many gyms also offer "gym to crag" education, or you can hire a guide service to learn these skills in a controlled environment with expert feedback.

If there are drop-in anchor hooks (mussy hooks) or carabiners on the anchors, no threading or knot untying is required for cleaning. (This may seem obvious, but I've often seen people do it, and it adds unnecessary risk for the climber.) If you are cleaning after leading, simply clip the hooks/carabiners at the anchors. If you are cleaning after top-roping, clip direct into the anchors as a backup, and then, instead of threading, just place the rope into the hooks/carabiners and transition back to your belayer. In both cases, do your normal checks before cleaning any of your own gear and lowering off the anchor system.

Tip #1: Consider the orientation of the anchors. When you are threading or clipping anchors, think about which side of the anchors you want to be on while lowering. Try to clip the anchors in a way that minimizes rope-on-rope contact during the lowering process. For example, if your belayer is down to your right, you should clip or thread the anchors so you lower on the left side.

Tip #2: Clean the anchors from an adjacent route. If you are climbing a series of routes side by side and have enough draws, you may be able to lower from draws at the anchors of one route and then clean them after climbing an adjacent route. This is easier on closely spaced routes where the anchor of the second route is higher than the previous route. Be sure you understand the implications of any fall if you have to scramble/traverse to reach your gear.

CLEANING THE DRAWS

When cleaning any route, take your time and use good judgment. Before removing each draw, think about how the system will change. The lowering climber is the pendulum, and the anchor location is the pivot point. When each draw is removed, the cleaning climber will swing toward and often past the pivot point, depending on friction and other variables in the system. Be aware of this directional swing and any hazards for both the swinging climber and the rope above, which can rub over edges or snag on bushes or rocks that may be loose.

If the route is not very steep—up to vertical or slightly overhanging—and the bolts lie directly under the anchor, cleaning while lowering is simple. Ask the belayer to hold you at each bolt and unclip the draw. It's often easier to unclip the bolt end of the draw first and then remove the draw from the rope.

TRAM TECHNIQUE

When a route is very overhanging or the line of bolts and draws is not directly below the anchor, the tram technique (a.k.a. trolley or rail car technique) becomes very useful. When tramming, the lowering climber gets help from the belayer's side of the rope to reach the next draw. It also helps to control the pendulum swing when each draw is cleaned on the route.

Clip the straight-gate side of a draw to your harness belay loop and clip the rope side of the draw to the belayer's rope. Have your belayer lower you until you are roughly even with or slightly below the next draw. With your belayer keeping you tight, pull on the belayer's rope to move in the direction of the next draw. On really steep routes, it can help to face away from the wall in a horizontal body position and pull in

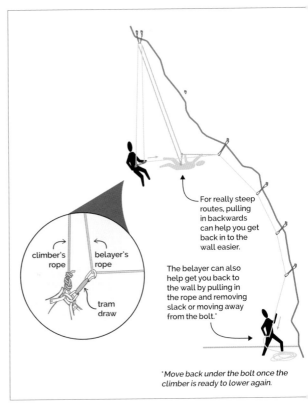

climber's rope

belayer's rope

tram draw

For really steep routes, pulling in backwards can help you get back in to the wall easier.

The belayer can also help get you back to the wall by pulling in the rope and removing slack or moving away from the bolt.*

*Move back under the bolt once the climber is ready to lower again.

PRESERVING THE FIRST BOLT

Bolts are generally stronger under shear force (when forces are pulling perpendicular to the wall) than when forces are pulling straight out from the wall. But we often create outward force when belaying and cleaning, especially at the first bolt. This outward force can be reduced by belaying directly under the first bolt instead of away from the wall. This is especially important when the rock is less solid, like the sandstone of the desert Southwest, Red Rock, Garden of the Gods, and the Red River Gorge.

head first–anyone who has crossed a Tyrolean traverse will be familiar with this technique.

While you are lowering on the tram, your belayer can assist you into the wall by pulling or "sitting" on the rope. This is easier when the climber is lighter than the belayer, and an assisted-braking device will help the belayer make rapid adjustments and lock off the belay rope. Depending on the route and the belay area, the belayer also may be able to take in rope by moving away from the first bolt. Be sure to move back under the first bolt once the climber has removed the draw and is ready to continue lowering.

Removing each draw on steep or traversing routes can be difficult due to the directional forces the rope puts on the draw. When you lower to the next draw on the wall, assess the situation before removing it. It can help to grab the dogbone of the draw or heel hook the belayer's side of the rope below the draw for stability while you work out how to clean the draw. Sometimes you need to get back on the route like you are climbing to remove the draw from the wall. Another option is a quick dead-point move: With one hand holding the gate clipped to the bolt in the open position and the other hand on the dogbone, pull yourself in quickly and work the carabiner off the bolt before gravity forces you to re-weight the tram.

If you use the tram technique, only unclip the tram draw from the belayer's rope while you are close to the wall (typically when you have clipped in direct to a bolt). If you unclip while you're dangling far from the wall and the belay strand is at a sharp angle, slack will be introduced to the system and you will drop suddenly. This can be very dangerous when you're close to the ground.

FIXED LOWERING GEAR

Some routes will be equipped with one or more permadraws or carabiners to help with cleaning. This gear serves as a directional for the lowering climber, changing the pivot point from the anchors to this gear.

In the case of a permadraw, you'll likely have clipped the permadraw for protection while leading. When you're lowering, swap out the belayer's side of the rope with your side (the lowering climber's side).

If there's a single carabiner left mid-route for cleaning, try to place your own draw *under* the fixed carabiner while leading, so your draw is optimally positioned for the load of a fall. Then, while lowering, place your strand of the rope in the carabiner before you remove your draw from this bolt.

Going in direct to the bolt can help with these rope transitions. Always assess fixed gear for any signs of excessive wear or sharp edges. And don't assume a carabiner left on a route is abandoned gear that you can take!

THE BOTTOM DRAW

Cleaning the last draw while lowering on a steep route is potentially dangerous. The swing for the cleaning climber is typically greatest at the bottom of the route, and since the climber is low to the ground, hazards like trees and rocks are more likely to be relevant. A misstep at this stage can endanger the belayer as well. Use the following steps to keep you and your belayer safe:

- **Go in direct.** Grab the draw connected to the bolt, unclip your tram draw from the belayer's rope, and clip it into either carabiner on the draw clipped to the bolt. Alternatively, you can use another draw or sling—anything to connect your belay loop to the draw or bolt on the wall. Be mindful of which side of the belayer's rope you want to be on to prevent the rope from twisting between you and the anchors or around the gear.
- **Assess the situation.** You are in straight, so take some time to think about the trajectory you will take once removing this draw. Are there obstacles? Consider lowering and then removing the last draw from the ground (*see next section*).
- **Free your belayer.** Always unclip the belayer's rope so you don't take them for a ride when you swing. Have your belayer give you a little slack (you are clipped in direct) and remove the belayer's strand of rope from any draws connecting the belayer to you or the wall. Unless you decide to leave the lowest draw in place, the belayer's rope should be running straight to the anchor above. Once free, they can find a good position for the final lower (*see sidebar on next page*).
- **Remove all slack.** The belayer must take all the slack out of the

Always free your belayer before removing the last draw from the route. If you are connected to the belayer's side of the rope, you could drag them into obstacles when you swing.

system and should take a crouched stance. (The tighter the rope, the better.) As the cleaning climber, confirm that all the slack and stretch is out of the system by pulling up and verifying your weight is 100 percent on the rope and no longer on the first draw.

- **Take the swing.** At this point, you are ready to remove the draw and release from the wall. Enjoy the ride! Be sure to look where you are swinging to address any obstacles.
- **Ask to be lowered.** Finishing the lower while the climber is swinging can be tricky for the belayer. Make sure there are no twists or snags in the rope. (Nothing is worse for the climber than having the rope get stuck in the belay device with the climber hurtling over boulders and into bushes.) The lower may need to be timed to land the climber in a certain location. This takes practice. There's typically no rush to get them to the ground; let them swing a few times to reduce the magnitude of the swing.
- **Beware of rope length.** Lowering from an overhanging or traversing route may take more rope than expected, especially if the lowered climber ends up down a hill. Always close the system by tying a stopper knot or tying in the belayer!

*Tip #1: **Clean the first bolt while clipped direct to the second bolt.*** This keeps you higher on the route before taking the final swing. Typically, early bolts on a climb are spaced closer together to reduce the risk of a ground fall. If this is the case, go in straight to the second bolt and reach down to retrieve the draw on the first bolt. Then, follow all the above steps before taking the swing. This technique can be used anywhere on a route where you can reach multiple draws from a single location. The less you swing, the faster you can clean!

*Tip #2: **Climb up after cleaning.*** If the bottom of the route is relatively easy,

BELAYER POSITIONING

When the climber takes the swing after cleaning the final draw, the belayer can be lifted into the air by the force of the swinging climber. This is especially true when the belayer is lighter than the climber. For the belayer, several steps will ensure a safe conclusion to the lower:

- Make sure you are free from your climber before they remove the last draw off the route.
- Move underneath the anchors to minimize any swing if you are lifted off the ground.
- Think about where the climber is going to swing and make sure your side of the rope is not in their way.
- Remove the slack and stretch from the system and take a crouched position before the climber releases from the wall. That way, if the force of the swing is enough to pull you up, there is room to stand before being lifted off the ground. It is also helpful to brace against a rock or tree.

It's often useful to clean the lowest draw on a route from above. Clip in direct to the second bolt (note the long tether), reach down to unclip the first draw, and then clean the second draw. *Johnny Nowell*

consider climbing some of the route after retrieving the draws to lessen the swing.

Tip #3: Leave a directional. Temporarily leave a draw somewhere mid-route and use it as a directional to clean the bottom half of the route. (This can be especially helpful for routes that overhang or traverse more in the upper section.) First, clean the top draws of the route until there's a logical place to leave a directional. Replace the belayer's side of the rope in this draw with your side of the rope, then continue to lower and clean the draws below the directional. When you're done, climb back up to the directional to clean this draw and swing off. This can also help protect the rope if it's running over a bulge or edge every time you clean a draw and swing off.

REMOVE THE LOWEST DRAW FROM THE GROUND

An easy way to finish cleaning a steep route is to leave the bottom draw clipped and lower to the ground, then retrieve this last draw from the ground. This is a good tactic when the swing for the cleaning climber is unsafe or would leave the climber in an undesirable position once lowered (e.g., hanging over a pond or a drop-off).

Here are two options for completing the lower with the first draw left in place:

(1) Keep your tram draw clipped to the rope *above* the draw on the first bolt, and then ask the belayer to lower you to the ground. One benefit of this option is efficiency. No ropes are switched, and the belayer doesn't need to move. However, the climber will land well out from the cliff, so, while it eliminates the swing, it may not be desirable for situations with hazards directly underneath the anchors. In addition, the climber must not remove the tram during the lower. Doing so will instantaneously introduce rope slack and drop the climber.

(2) Option two is to swap the belayer's rope in the last draw with the climber's side of the rope. This method is especially useful in situations where there are obstacles or hazards directly underneath the anchors. It can be helpful to clip in direct to the

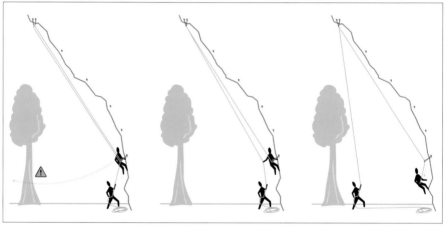

[Top] To avoid a potentially dangerous swing from the lowest bolt, one option is to maintain the tram while the belayer lowers you all the way down. Never unclip the tram until you're on the ground. [Bottom] Another option is to replace the belayer's side of the rope at the first draw with your side. Clip in direct to make the switch, and reposition the belayer before lowering.

bolt before swapping the ropes. Be mindful of which side of the belayer's rope you want to be on to keep the rope from getting twisted between you and the anchors.

Now you just have to retrieve the first quickdraw. If the bottom of the route is easy and the bolt isn't too high, the climber or belayer can simply boulder up and get the first draw. (Be mindful of rock quality, as well as the quality of the landing in case of a fall.) Or, the draw can be retrieved using most modern stick clips. The Superclip, Beta Stick, Squid, and homemade stick clips utilizing a metal spring clamp all can be used to both place and remove a draw from a route. Check YouTube to learn how to use these tools. If you don't have a stick clip, try to borrow one or see if a nearby climbing party with one can help you remove the draw. Climbers are typically really good about helping fellow climbers stay safe. Especially if you ask nicely.

If a stick clip is not available, the wall side carabiner on the first draw can be taped open (go in direct to the first bolt and have your belayer toss you the tape). Be aware that the gate will be open while you are lowering–use caution and avoid movement that would jostle the draw while lowering. Once on the ground, shake the rope going to the draw until it pops off the first bolt or use a stick to push the draw off the bolt. This tape trick works best with a keylock carabiner clipped to the first bolt.

CLEAN ON TOP-ROPE

With the guidance in this article, most climbs can be safely cleaned by lowering after leading. There are exceptions: routes with long traverses close to the ground, for example, or ones where the base area has enough obstacles that any swing will be dangerous. If a route seems unsafe or impractical to clean while lowering, you can always clean by following on top-rope.

The decision to clean the route on top-rope should be made before the leader leaves the ground, so the upper anchor can be equipped properly for top-roping. The cleaning climber

A stick clip can be used to remove the first quickdraw from a route. *Johnny Nowell*

should tie into the rope that's clipped into the draws. It's also a good idea to pre-stretch the rope to better protect a low top-rope fall. Before leaving the ground, have the belayer take out all the slack and sit on the rope. (The climber can weight the rope as well.) Keep the slack out of the rope as the climber steps up to the wall. Now, you are ready to climb–and as a bonus, you've pretested your knot!

GET OUT AND PRACTICE

Any climber new to cleaning steep routes should start with gently overhanging climbs to gain experience in a lower risk environment, ideally with an experienced mentor. You can also hire a guide service and let them know you want to learn how to clean overhanging routes. This may require a special trip to the Red, Rifle, or another area that has a large concentration of steep climbing. It's a tough life.

Don't forget that all those super-helpful lowering hooks and permadraws are maintained by your fellow climbers and local climbing organizations. Be a hero at the crag, ready to replace worn gear with a few steel carabiners stashed in your pack. Or donate to the LCO. Do your part to keep climbing fun, safe, and epic-free.

Lindsay Auble is a recreational climber, a professional engineer, and a volunteer editor for this publication. She spends the spring and fall in the Red River Gorge, climbing with strong and experienced mentors on the steep climbs of the South.

The north face of Pioneer Peak in winter, rising more than 5,000 vertical feet. The lower route line is shown, with (X) marking the spot where two climbers were avalanched. *Cecil Sanders*

ALASKA

AVALANCHES | Poor Position, Rope Cut, Anchor Tether Failure
Chugach Mountains, Pioneer Peak

Pioneer Peak looms over the Knik River, northeast of Anchorage. The north face is a broad pyramid laced with gullies, starting at 500 feet above sea level and rising to the summit at 6,398 feet. The classic route follows a direct line to the summit ridge, beginning with 20° slopes and gradually steepening to about 60°. Along the way are a couple of steeper ice pitches, the first at about 1,000 feet into the route and the second at about 4,000 feet.

Fallon Connolly, 26, and Simon Frez-Albrecht, age 28 (both experienced climbers), started up the face at 5:45 a.m. on April 15. It had been 37°F at the car. After about an hour, they neared the first technical pitch (30 meters, WI3). Above this, they unroped and continued snow climbing for about two hours.The gully ramped up to about 50° shortly before the upper technical pitch.

Fallon observed signs of what appeared to be fairly recent avalanches on the gully walls. Simon had checked the weather stations in Hatcher Pass, about 25 miles away as the crow flies, for recent nighttime temperatures, and found they had been below freezing above roughly 3,000 feet the last couple of nights. The forecast for Palmer (halfway between Hatcher and Pioneer at 250 feet above sea level) was for a daytime high in the low 40s and rain in the afternoon. Simon figured the bottom half of the route would be above freezing, but anticipated the upper face could have good névé conditions. Indeed, the snow kept getting better and firmer the higher they got, but they later determined this was from being buffed by avalanches, not frozen solid.

Shortly before entering a pinch leading to the upper ice pitch, both heard/sensed a faint booming-rumbling sound or sensation that made them pause. They discussed it briefly. Could it be a distant sonic boom from military jets? Noise from the firing range? A snow whumph? After another minute, Fallon identified a similar sound/feeling, but they agreed to continue upward. They later deduced these had been distant avalanches on another aspect of the mountain.

Simon was about 50 feet ahead of Fallon and had nearly reached a position to anchor for the upper ice pitch when he noticed a very small (D0.5 or D1) wet loose avalanche come tumbling over the ice above. He yelled down to warn Fallon. Simon was standing to one side of the gully, and it didn't hit him, but it all washed directly over Fallon; she planted both tools firmly and put her head down to let the snow pass. They estimated the flow lasted 60 seconds.

After the flow stopped, Fallon continued up to where Simon was waiting and they moved together perhaps 50 feet up and to the opposite side of the gully, where there were some obvious cracks in the rock. Around 11:15 to 11:30, Simon dug some snow out and found a placement for a perfect number 2 Camalot, which he clipped into while placing a number 4 Black Diamond Stopper in the crack formed by a chockstone about a foot above. Simon equalized the two pieces with a 60cm Dyneema sling. They both clipped in, Fallon using an 8mm Dyneema runner girth-hitched through both hardpoints on her harness. Given what they had observed, they agreed it would be prudent to descend from this point.

To build a bail anchor, they dug snow out of a horizontal seam about two feet below the Stopper and forced a knifeblade piton in about halfway before it began deforming. Simon tied off the blade with 6mm cord and equalized it with the nut, intentionally shifting slightly more force to nut. He bounce-tested the anchor and then set up their brand-new 7.8mm ropes for a rappel, with the pink rope threaded through the masterpoint and tied to the green rope with a single offset overhand and a single overhand "backup." Fallon pre-rigged her device on the rappel ropes but did not install a friction-hitch backup. The number 2 Camalot was clipped to the ropes as a backup with a non-locker on a 60cm sling. Fallon remained clipped to the cord masterpoint with a locking carabiner as Simon began to rappel, using an Edelrid Giga Jul. When Simon was about halfway down, Fallon yelled to warn of an avalanche coming over the ice pitch above.

When Fallon saw the avalanche, she grabbed her tether near the carabiner and pulled close to the rock wall, keeping as much of her weight on her feet as she could. She was looking over her shoulder to see when the debris flow would stop when she was hit in the face by a block. She was knocked off her feet and was hanging fully from her tether, getting buffeted by debris. Her gloves disappeared, and her glasses fell off. She reached for the anchor to try to pull herself back upright but couldn't grab anything.

At around this point, the pink rope broke. (The climbers later deduced it was cut by an edge of the rock near the anchor.) However, the knot joining the two ropes jammed in Fallon's pre-rigged rappel device, keeping the green rope attached to the anchor via her belay device and her tether. At this point, Simon was fully hanging from the belay device rigged on Fallon's belay loop.

Simon had assumed the avalanche would be small, like the earlier one, so he tried moving to the side of the gully. However, debris almost immediately pulled him into the fall line, knocked him off his feet, and flowed over him. He felt rope slipping through his gloved brake hand and tried to hold on, but then had his hand knocked off the ropes and felt that he was sliding down the ropes in halting jerks. Eventually he came to a hard stop on the rope but kept getting pummeled. After one to three minutes, the flow slowed and then stopped. Simon stood up and found that a tangle in the green rope had jammed in his belay device, stopping him from going further. The pink rope was piled in a mess near him.

Once Simon stood up and unweighted the rope, Fallon got back on her feet and immediately noticed the pink rope had been cut. She grabbed the green rope and clipped it through the carabiner on the number 2 Camalot, but did not use a knot to anchor it. Simon and Fallon began trying to communicate—Simon yelling to fix the green rope and hurry down, Fallon not hearing clearly what he was saying. As Fallon inspected the anchor, the next rumble started above.

The second avalanche knocked Fallon off her feet, and instantly she knew she was falling. She tumbled down the slope in the debris, totally disoriented. Simon saw the second flow beginning to spill over the ice pitch and hurried to get behind a rock outcrop in the middle of the gully. A small, roof-shaped feature protected him as the debris flowed past, but then he was plucked from his stance by tugging on his harness. Almost immediately he understood that Fallon had come detached from the anchor and was falling below him. He tumbled head over heels down the slope until finally he was able to dig in his heels and stop after about 100 feet. Fallon had fallen 300 to 400 feet from the anchor to where she stopped.

The two yelled back and forth again, and Fallon started moving onto a small rib of rock outcrops in the middle of the gully. Simon untangled his ice tools from the clippers on his harness and hurriedly downclimbed and slid the 45° slope to Fallon. He noticed pain in his ribs on the right side during certain motions, but otherwise didn't notice any significant injuries. When Simon reached her, she was obviously in distress, and told him that she had lost her gloves, helmet, and ice tools. Her beacon had been torn out of the thigh pocket of her Gore-Tex pants. She got a second pair of gloves out of her backpack and moved off the rock toward Simon, who gave her one of his tools. He hurried Fallon to shelter in the lee of a larger rock outcrop just below them, providing a short rope for security.

Behind the rock outcrop, they caught their breath and formulated a plan. A raised area of the snowfield on the other side of a large debris path led into a more defined rib sticking out between gullies farther down the mountain. They aimed to stay on this high point as they worked their way down the mountain. After listening carefully for the rumbling of another avalanche, they began to hurry across the gully to the high point. Simon was a few feet uphill of Fallon, keeping her on a short rope as they moved together. Getting on the high point, they again paused to catch their breath before continuing down. They were comforted by the rib gaining prominence as they descended, as well as the increased density of alders and spruce trees.

In the areas unaffected by the avalanches, they found knee- to hip-deep post-holing in the soft snow. As they got lower into the dense alders, the snowpack was thinner, and Fallon kicked off several collapses and small avalanches, sliding on a saturated layer essentially at the ground interface. Eventually the rib began to cliff out, so they made a 20-meter rappel off a clump of alders. More downclimbing through 45° alder slopes brought them to the anchor at the top of the first belayed pitch. They added a piton to the anchor, rigged what was left of their rope for a rappel, and then were able to walk down to the road. They reached the car at 4:45 p.m.; the temperature was 41°F and light rain was falling.

Simon's injuries included several rope burns and crampon pokes, a bruised rib, a strained left bicep and wrist, and other pain and stiffness. Fallon had painful (probably broken) ribs on the lower left side, badly bruised and swollen knees, two black eyes and a swollen lip, and cuts and soreness at various other points all over her body. (Sources: Simon Frez-Albrecht and Fallon Connolly.)

ANALYSIS

Reviewing incidents in the past, I (Simon) could point to obvious red flags or glaring mistakes in decision-making. The clues that we missed this time were more subtle, and therefore it's harder to draw conclusions about what to do better next time.

Apart from not going on the face at all or turning back in the first hour, we could not have been more fortunate with our timing. If we had been slower or had turned around when we first heard/sensed the ominous noise, we likely would have been unroped and right in the gun barrel when the slides hit, and we could have been swept to the bottom of the face. If we had been faster, I would have been leading the upper ice pitch, taking a lead fall as well as a pummeling.

Even though this is one of our local mountains, we had been away for the past two weeks, so were out of touch with the snowpack and weather patterns. The human factor known as "scarcity" made me want to jump onto the face—I suspected this might be the last day of the spring season to climb the route. We felt we had pieced together enough information to make an informed decision. I suspected the shed cycle had already happened in the previous warm, sunny days, so there wouldn't be a significant amount of loose/available snow left on the mountain to slide onto us. I didn't consider that the freezing at night had been enough to keep the snow locked in place, poised above us.

Probably the single most obvious clue we missed was that it had stayed cloudy the night before our climb, preventing the radiant cooling that had dropped night-time temps in the previous days. This kept the snowpack wet and near the tipping point when the weak sun struck the face for a couple of hours through the clouds.

In the moments leading up to the avalanche, we felt good that we were heading down, heeding the warning signal sent by the small wet sluff. We didn't yet understand that this sluff was the *last* of several subtle warnings telling us that this was not a good day to be climbing on Pioneer.

I went back up about 10 days later when we had another spell of freezing nights. (This time the snow was crunchy underfoot right from the car.) I wanted to investigate the anchor to see why we had come off, but didn't find much in the way of answers. The nut was firmly locked in place, with that leg of the anchor cord and the masterpoint still in good condition; the cord that I had tied off on the piton had been cut. The Camalot above was still in place, with the sling and non-locker dangling from it, slightly deformed. Fallon's tether and the locking carabiner came down with her when she fell. Why had she come unclipped from the anchor? The only conclusion we can draw is that the screw-gate locker with which Fallon clipped her tether to the masterpoint must have jiggled to the unlocked position during the first avalanche.

[Left] **Post-avalanche view of the anchor on Pioneer Peak. The anchor was mostly intact; only the cord to the piton had failed.** [Right] **The rope likely was cut by sawing against a sharp rock edge.** *Simon Frez-Albrecht*

Then, when she unweighted the tether, the locker must have shifted into a position where it could unclip itself when the second avalanche pushed her back onto her tether.

As I inspected the anchor, I identified a sharp rock edge below and to the side that matched up with where the rope had been cut. We concluded that the large oscillations and force on the rope during the avalanche, as it loaded over a sharp edge of rock, had cut the rope.

Over the last year or two, I have been making a conscious effort to increase my safety margin while climbing. This includes tying knots in the ends of ropes during rappels, using a rappel backup, and using autolocking carabiners and assisted braking belay devices more often. I had recently been toying with pre-rigging rappel devices as well, but was not doing this consistently. For whatever reason, this was one of those times we pre-rigged Fallon's belay device on the rope, and by snagging the knot joining the ropes after our pink rope cut, it happened to keep me alive. (*Source: Simon Frez-Albrecht.*)

LEADER FALL ON ROCK | Flipped Upside Down
Hatcher Pass, The Monolith

On July 14, I met up with two partners to climb some trad routes in Hatcher Pass. I had been leading trad for more than four years and regularly traveled outside of Alaska to get practice outside of our very short summer climbing season.

After warming up on an easy climb, we moved over to a two-pitch 5.9+ route called Orangutan Overhang that I had not climbed before. I led the first pitch clean and built an anchor on the ledge between the pitches. I brought up my followers, and we discussed whether to continue up the second pitch, which you could not see from the ground. It looked slightly easier than the first pitch, and I decided to head up.

The pitch started in a corner that protected well and felt a bit steeper than it looked. I got in a few pieces of gear before reaching a large chockstone that looked and felt loose. I moved past it quickly and did not protect close to it due to concern about dislodging it. I found myself on a thin ledge that traversed right to a roof. I found a very small horizontal placement (black Totem Cam, the smallest in their range) before the move to the right. It wasn't a great placement, but there was mud and water running in the larger crack under the roof (typical for this area), and I didn't think I could safely protect there.

I reached a pretty comfortable stance to check out the moves over the roof. There was a short hand crack right above the roof and what looked like an OK high-step on the right side. I checked that my left hand felt solid in the jam and then moved my right foot up to the high-step. I don't recall how I fell, but I pretty much immediately flipped upside down. I have some recollection of my head (and helmet!) impacting the rock, after which the black Totem pulled out and I slid down the face. I fell another 20-plus feet before my other gear held me and I came to a stop close to the belay ledge.

I stood upright on the ledge to try to assess the situation. I had trouble speaking and had to hold my neck stable to be able to breathe comfortably, so I lay down in the recovery position and kept my neck supported out of concern about a spinal cord injury.

One of my partners rappelled the first pitch, activated my personal locator beacon (PLB), and helped coordinate rescue support. He was able to send up water, warm layers, etc., while my second partner stayed on the ledge with me. At close to 9 p.m., I was rescued by helicopter from the ledge.

At the hospital, I was diagnosed with multiple fractures to my C1 vertebra, an occipital skull fracture, multiple fractures to my upper jaw, cheekbones, and nose, and a broken molar. A couple of weeks later, we found that I had a full tear to my scapholunate ligament in my left hand and a partial tear to my MCL on my left knee. Fortunately, I have recovered well except for some loss of range of motion in my neck and left wrist.

Helmet damaged in the Hatcher Pass fall.
Katherine Cooper

ANALYSIS

I was aware that I didn't have good protection nearby (and even verbally noted that to my belayer), but decided to try the move anyway. I was accustomed to being a little above my gear, especially on various alpine climbs that I've done. I expected the gear that was good to keep me off the ground—which it did—but I grossly misjudged the fall risk in that spot. I just didn't consider that I might be flipped upside down in the fall. (All I can think is that my high right foot put my center of balance in a weird place.) Unfortunately, I think I may have been just as injured if the piece had not pulled—my gear was too far down and left of my fall line.

I also think that while I was feeling physically strong, my technique (specifically footwork) might have been worse than usual due to the gym closure earlier in the year. I had climbed very little since the COVID-19 closures in early March. (*Source: Katherine Cooper.*)

CALIFORNIA

MT. SHASTA ANNUAL SUMMARY
Mt. Shasta and Castle Crags Wilderness

The number of accidents and searches on Mt. Shasta was down from the last couple of seasons, most likely due to COVID-19 and the associated forest closure and stay-at-home orders, which kept people off the mountain for a while. In 2020, the U.S. Forest Service (USFS) sold 4,633 summit passes, compared with the 20-year average of 6,467. In total, there were 12 search and rescue incidents on Mt. Shasta (not all involving climbing), while the average is 20 per year. Unfortunately, one of the accidents resulted in a fatality. Below are details of some of the incidents.

On Monday, March 2, a 50-year-old male climber contacted the USFS climbing rangers looking for assistance in recovering his tent and belongings from Lake Helen. He had been planning a solo, two-day winter climb of the Avalanche Gulch route, with a camp at Lake Helen, but cold and strong wind made for a challenging experience setting up his tent. He turned back and abandoned the majority of his gear, and he reported having severe frostbite on his fingers when he returned home. The climber's tent was recovered the next day, tangled in the rocks a few hundred feet below Lake Helen. Setting up a tent in difficult conditions is an often underestimated skill in winter mountaineering.

On June 14, a climber called 911 reporting severe right shoulder pain after a self-arrest attempt while glissading above Lake Helen. The climber had been descending after a successful summit with a partner and a guide. While glissading, she began going too fast and attempted to self-arrest, but the axe grabbed the snow in such a way that injured her shoulder. She attempted to hike down, but the pain was unbearable, and she called for help. The decision was made to evacuate her by helicopter.

Late in the afternoon on June 21, rangers received information about an injured climber at 11,000 feet on the west face route. When rangers arrived on scene, an assessment revealed possible broken ribs and breathing complications on the right side of the chest. The reporting party stated the climber had fallen while downclimbing a 50° slope, losing control and colliding with a rock garden at the bottom. The climber was extracted via helicopter.

Two falls in late June occurred in the same general location (circled) on Mt. Shasta's west face route. *Nick Meyers | USFS*

A week later, a 55-year-old climber also slipped and fell while descending the same general area on the west face. The climber had crampons on and an ice axe in his hand when he slipped and slid 400 feet, colliding with an exposed rock patch at the bottom of the snow slope. His partner stated that the man was speaking in German (he usually speaks English) and was alert and oriented only to his name.

When rangers arrived, a head-to-toe assessment revealed facial trauma, black-and-blue eyes, and pain in the right shoulder and upper thoracic spine. The patient was wearing a helmet. Two nearby climbers hiked up to help, and one was instructed to hold C-spine. It was determined to be unsafe to carry the patient without a litter, so rangers hiked in a SKED litter from the helicopter landing zone in Hidden Valley. The patient was packaged in the SKED and carried down across rock and snow to the Hidden Valley camp, where he was loaded into a helicopter for transport to the hospital.

On July 5, a climber who had summited via the Avalanche Gulch route got off route during his descent and headed onto the Whitney Glacier. The 47-year-old was equipped with crampons and a single trekking pole. After the recent low-precipitation winters, the Whitney Glacier is a jumbled mess of rock, ice, and crevasses. The climber, now marooned on an island of rocks at about 13,000 feet, reported that "moving off the rock pile may cost him his life." Yet, while waiting for rescue, the climber decided to try and descend on his own, haphazardly glissading on a path that took him over a crevasse and onto a snow bridge in another crevasse. During his fall, the climber injured his neck and nose. He climbed out of the crevasse and began to descend again, this time avoiding crevasses, before stopping near 11,000 feet. The helicopter and rescuers redirected after locating the climber's *new* position, and rangers arrived on scene at 8 p.m. and helped the climber to the landing zone at 10,400 feet.

On September 25, Chelsey Klein and Jeffrey Sutton started from the Northgate trailhead and set up camp two miles up the trail as the sun began to set. The next morning, they attempted to climb the Hotlum-Bolam Ridge. Approximately eight hours into their day, the pair decided to descend from a high point near 13,000 feet. In late afternoon, at about 12,000 feet, they realized they had deviated from their ascent route. They put on crampons, got out their ice axes, and attempted to traverse across the western reaches of the Hotlum Glacier to regain the

Rangers' makeshift bivouac with meager shelter from rockfall during an extended rescue in the Trinity Chutes area. *Nick Meyers | USFS*

lateral moraine. As they traversed, Sutton slipped and fell, tumbling a few hundred feet down the very icy slope. Conditions were such that self-arrest was impossible.

Klein called 911 and reported that Sutton was unconscious. After a few minutes he began to move and attempted to stand up, but then slipped a second time and fell out of view. Late that night, with assistance from California National Guard, Klein was rescued by helicopter. The crew returned to search for Sutton, but was unable to locate him. Two climbing rangers were inserted to 8,600 feet, and additional searchers began hiking from Northgate trailhead. At sunrise, rangers began searching the glacier and located Sutton, who was deceased.

On October 5, a 23-year-old climber slipped and fell from 12,500 feet in the middle of the Trinity Chutes in Avalanche Gulch. At this time of the year, the south side of the mountain was completely devoid of snow, and the Trinity Chutes is one of the most rockfall-prone portions of the mountain. The climber called 911 and reported a chief complaint of two broken ankles.

With little time left in the day, a helicopter crew inserted two rangers to Helen Lake. The plan was to move the climber to a safer location for the night, preparing for a hoist the following morning. Rangers arrived on scene and found multiple lacerations head to toe (no helmet), a severe open thumb injury, possible broken ribs and broken left ankle, and possible dislocated right ankle. Rangers moved the climber to a location away from the active rockfall, behind a moderate sized boulder on the 35° to 40° slope. It was now dark, and they determined it would be unsafe to haul the climber down the slope any further. The patient was covered in emergency blankets and warm garments, and the rangers took cover from the ongoing rockfall behind some small boulders.

In the early morning, California Highway Patrol's H-14 helicopter arrived on scene. There was pressure to get the patient to a lower elevation, as the CHP crew were not confident they could hoist the patient from this elevation. However, after stripping the helicopter of extraneous equipment and burning off fuel, they were able to conduct the hoist near maximum power. All rescue personnel made it off the mountain safely.

ANALYSIS

The snowpack on Shasta was far below the historic average, which meant the safest climbing conditions were earlier in the spring than usual and didn't last long—especially since the USFS closed the mountain above 10,000 feet from April 23 to May 15 because of concerns related to the pandemic. When the closure lifted, Shasta received heavy visitation, and some climbers, despite warnings, gave the mountain a go all season long. As the snow melted out, there was a gradual increase in rockfall and icy snow surfaces, and slip-and-fall consequences were greatly exacerbated by falls that terminated into boulders.

As usual, there were a couple of searches for climbers who were unfamiliar with the terrain, separated from their group, did not have navigation tools, and/or got lost in poor weather or limited visibility.

Mt. Shasta is often described as a "beginner" mountaineering objective, but the technical requirements should not be understated. Climbers looking to grow their mountaineering skills should strongly consider hiring a guide who can supervise the practice of new skills and add a margin of safety. (*Mt. Shasta Climbing Ranger Report and 2020 Search and Rescue Incident Narratives.*)

INCORRECT TIE-IN | Distraction
Yosemite National Park, Five & Dime Cliff

On June 4, Alex and Jane (pseudonyms) started their afternoon of climbing on Mockery, a bolted 5.8 route. Jane began leading, but a few bolts up she asked to get lowered. The climbers switched roles and Alex ascended the route to the bolted anchor. He clipped the rope through two alpine quickdraws for a top-rope anchor, and Jane began to lower him. She reported that Alex asked her to "stop" or "hold on" about halfway to the ground (approximately 35 feet). He appeared to be manipulating something on his harness and then suddenly fell to the ground.

Rangers responded and provided emergency medical care (Alex had a fractured femur and other injuries), then performed a low-angle evacuation to transport him to a park ambulance.

ANALYSIS

During the investigation, rangers inspected the route and climbing gear. The climbers' rope was still hanging from the anchor, with a properly tied figure-eight follow-through knot jammed against the carabiners clipped to the slings. The knot was not tied to anything. The ranger performing medical care on Alex found all his buckles intact and properly secured when removing the harness. The harness generally seemed to be in good condition. The only exception was that the small, non-load-bearing "keeper loop," below the bottom "hard point" between the two leg loops, was undone.

The evidence suggests Alex may have been distracted while tying in and tied a correct knot to an incorrect place on the harness, threading the rope through the keeper loop instead of the reinforced hard points of the harness. Alex tied in with the lead rope still clipped into a couple of bolts above him, and the rope may have obscured the incorrect tie-in. He may have noticed something amiss while lowering and might have been manipulating the harness when the loop came undone.

Although these two had climbed together before, they were not regular partners. They reported that buddy checks were performed prior to beginning this climb. Nonetheless, this accident highlights the need for climbers to

A fallen leader's knot was discovered at the anchor, properly tied and clipped through the anchor, but not tied to anything. *NPS Photo*

guard against complacency during routine procedures like tie-ins and buddy checks. The error did not reveal itself until Alex weighted the system, after having climbed the full pitch. Alex is fortunate the accident did not occur right at the anchor.

Alex was wearing a helmet and commented, "I remember my head hitting tree branches or rock on the way down and being thankful I had it on." It is not uncommon for climbers to forego a helmet when climbing below their limit, especially on bolted routes. This incident highlights the importance of helmets even when the hazards seem minimal. (*Source: Yosemite National Park Climbing Rangers.*)

STRANDED | Rappel Error
Yosemite National Park, Leaning Tower

Two climbers attempting the West Face of Leaning Tower in June decided to descend after arriving at Ahwahnee Ledge (the top of the fourth pitch), due to excessive heat and sun. While rappelling the very overhanging first pitch with the haulbag, Climber A rappelled over a small roof and got too far away from the wall to reach the ledge at the bottom of the pitch, despite clipping some directionals during his descent. (The West Face route is approached by a ramp that traverses onto the face, so the first anchor is far above the ground.) Since the climber could not reach the ramp, he continued rappelling to a lower ledge. This ledge had no permanent anchor, and Climber A was not carrying the right pieces to construct a solid anchor. With no way to anchor the haul bag, he could not detach it from the ropes nor reascend the ropes to reach the ramp.

During their descent, the two climbers had called Yosemite Search and Rescue to

THE ART OF THE BAIL

Bailing off a steep route is a nearly inevitable outcome if you climb enough walls, so it's best to know how to get down safely before you find yourself dangling in space, wishing you knew what to do. Yosemite climbing rangers advise the following techniques for rappelling overhanging routes with a haulbag.

(1) The first person descending should rappel on a fixed single strand with a Grigri or a similar locking belay device, clipping *both* strands of the rappel ropes to directional pieces to keep them close to the wall. They should also carry equipment to reascend the fixed rope in case of getting too far from the wall or rappelling past the anchor.

(2) When the first person arrives at the lower anchor, they should feed out five to ten feet of slack rope, tie a knot with both ropes, and clip the knot to the anchor. This will close the system for the second rappeller and allow the second person to pull themselves into the wall to unclip directionals on their way down and to pull into the anchor at the end of the rappel.

(3) The second rappeller should untie the fixed strand from the upper anchor or undo any knot-blocks, and then rappel both strands as normal, using a tube-style device (such as an ATC) and a third-hand backup. They can unclip and clean the directional pieces as they descend. Note: The second person down should carry the team's heaviest gear (haulbag, etc.), because the tube-style device produces a smoother rappel than a Grigri. Plus, they should not have any reason to reascend the rope because it will be fixed to the lower anchor.

– Yosemite National Park Climbing Rangers

request some advice; climbing rangers were able to assist them over the phone with their first rappels, but soon decided to send SAR members to Leaning Tower in case further assistance was needed. When SAR members arrived, they fixed a rope and lowered it to Climber A, and he was able to leave his haul bag and jumar out. They then secured the team's rappel ropes to the ledge so the second climber could rappel directly to the approach ramp. The ropes and haulbag were retrieved later that day.

ANALYSIS

The Leaning Tower is one of the steepest big walls in North America, the lower half of which overhangs at an average angle of 110 degrees. The West Face has been the site of numerous rappelling difficulties, and while Climber A did utilize some directionals, he extended one piece with a long runner and soon found himself too far from the cliff to place more directional pieces. (*Source: Yosemite National Park Climbing Rangers.*)

LEADER FALL | Inadequate Protection, Communication
Yosemite National Park, Tuolumne Meadows

Some friends and I went to Lembert Dome on August 4. I was a moderately experienced sport and gym climber but new to trad climbing. One friend climbed the first pitch of Northwest Books (5.6) and left the gear for me so I could "pinkpoint" the route for my first trad lead. However, she did not place much gear: The bolt protecting the moves to the layback crack was clipped, and then she placed only two other pieces. These were maybe eight to 12 feet apart in a layback section. One of the alpine draws was also extended.

When I reached the point between the two pieces, I attempted to place a piece with the two random cams my friends had given me to "play with" for practice. (They thought they had sewed up the route and I wouldn't need gear for actual

YOSAR at work. *NPS Photo*

protection.) Neither of the pieces fit the crack. After a minute my foot slipped and I fell down the slab, rolling to the right. I impacted on my butt and continued rolling down the slab, hitting the back of my head. The foam lining of my helmet cracked.

My friends called 911, and Tuolumne Search and Rescue responded. They found tingling in my toes and tenderness in my lumbar spine, and due to the likelihood of a spinal injury, I was put into a full-body vacuum splint for the lower to the ground and carryout to the trail. At the hospital they found a fractured L1 vertebra. I was airlifted to Reno, Nevada, for possible spinal surgery, but luckily the fracture was stable and I only needed bracing. (*Source: Lynn Nguyen.*)

ANALYSIS

Yosemite Search and Rescue listed the following takeaways from this incident:

Wear a helmet: When Lynn fell, she flipped upside down and cracked her helmet; the outcome could have been much worse without one. Her foam-lined helmet helped protect her head from side and rear impact.

Be honest with yourself (and your partners): Lynn was told the first party would "sew up" the pitch and she would not need any other pieces to protect the climb. Later, her friend clarified that she had been "spooked" in the section after the first piece she placed, which is why she didn't stop to place more gear. If this had been communicated beforehand, Lynn might have made different decisions about the climb.

Falls on low-angle climbs can be consequential: Many of the climbs in Tuolumne Meadows are slabby, polished, and have sparse protection, and "beginner" routes often have numerous ledges. Climbers should be confident on the grade and style before leading these routes.

Gym routes are not comparable to outdoor routes: Climbing outside often requires skills not learned in the gym. Lynn mentioned not having much experience with laybacking or slab climbing. In addition, the grades do not always reflect the lack of protection, and original ("old school") ratings can feel difficult by today's standards.

Be cautious using preplaced gear: Each climber will have a different idea of how much gear should be placed and where it is placed. While learning to use traditional protection, consider practicing on top-rope; when ready to lead, bring extra pieces of protection. (*Source: Yosemite National Park Climbing Rangers.*)

FALL ON SNOW
Eastern Sierra, Mt. Humphreys, North Couloir

On June 10, Inyo SAR was notified of an overdue climber (age 59 and experienced) in the Mt. Humphreys area, west of Bishop. His wife reported that the climber's intended itinerary was to ascend the North Couloir (ice and snow up to 50°+) and descend the east ridge. Both are popular routes to summit.

Inyo SAR deployed three ground teams into the field by 8:30 a.m., heading for the east ridge, the North Couloir, and the approaches to the North Couloir. At 10 a.m., SAR learned that friends of the climber had begun to search the night before and had located the deceased climber near the bergschrund at the base of the North Couloir at approximately 12,000 feet. Inyo SAR and the California Highway Patrol helicopter completed the recovery of the subject by 12 p.m.

Using the climber's Strava track, Inyo SAR was able to determine that he had summited Mt. Humphreys, then returned via the North Couloir. It was obvious from the tracks that the climber had taken a fall from high in the couloir, hit rocks on the right side of the gully, slid over the bergschrund, and come to rest on a snow shelf just below the bergschrund. Judging from his tracks, he did not move again once he came to rest at the bergschrund.

ANALYSIS
We do not know the cause of the fall, but other parties reported hearing a large rockfall that morning, though no evidence of this was observed near the climber's up track or the slide marks. We also noted there was still abundant spring snow and it was a warm day. The footing in the couloir would have been treacherous as the day warmed up, and arresting a slip would have been difficult. The subject was well equipped for snow travel and carried a climbing rope. We cannot say with confidence that the snow conditions played a factor in the subject's fall, but we recommend alpine starts for better snow stability and to anticipate changing (worsening) snow conditions during the day. (*Source: Inyo County Search and Rescue.*)

LEADER FALL | Inadequate Equipment, Inexperience
Eastern Sierra, Pine Creek Canyon

On May 7 around 1:30 p.m., the Inyo County Sheriff's Office received notification of a fall victim with critical injuries in Pine Creek Canyon. The patient was reported to be near the top of an unnamed scrambling route, approximately 500 feet off the ground, above the gully at the right margin of the Mustache Wall. The two had just decided to rope up, and the leader had not yet placed any gear before he fell approximately 20 feet. The party was climbing without a full rack or full-length rope. Neither climber was wearing a helmet, and the patient sustained a severe head injury.

Inyo County Search and Rescue responded, and a team of two ascended a multi-pitch route to reach the party from below. Four additional members ascended 5th-class terrain on the southeast side of the same buttress, where they were able to top out and descend to the injured party with additional equipment. The injured climber was stabilized and lowered in stages to the base of the canyon.

The patient was a relatively inexperienced climber. The fall could have been prevented had the party been placing adequate gear to protect the climb. The patient's head injury could have been avoided, or ameliorated, if he had been wearing a helmet. (*Source: Inyo County Search and Rescue.*)

AVALANCHE | Late Start
Eastern Sierra, Independence Peak

Two skiers, male and female, both in their late 20s or early 30s, set out around 9:30 a.m. on April 29 to ski a prominent canyon on the northeast side of Independence Peak, near the Kearsarge Pass trailhead. After skinning up the chute for about 1.5 hours and gaining a couple of thousand feet, they stopped at about 11 a.m. on the edge of the gully to transition from skinning to booting. While they both had their packs off, they heard and then saw an "explosive fast-moving" avalanche release approximately 300 to 500 feet above them. With no time to react, both were caught up in the moving snow. The male was able to grab some rocks until the moving snow passed, but the female was carried out of sight down the canyon.

The male subject, now missing his skis and backpack, was able to move down the canyon and eventually found his partner (and half of a ski) on the skier's left edge of the debris, unburied but with rib and lower back injuries severe enough that she was unable to continue out. The avalanche had

Avalanche on Independence Peak. The approximate crown line and injured skier's location (X) after the slide are shown. The skier was carried about 1,000 vertical feet. *Inyo County SAR*

carried her approximately 1,000 feet.

The Inyo County Search and Rescue team was deployed along with resources from the California Highway Patrol (including CHP helicopter H40), Inyo County Sheriff, and CAL FIRE. The total response included over 40 personnel. Upon arrival of the SAR team, the snow safety officer and other team members evaluated conditions and concluded that the area continued to have high avalanche danger. The SAR team and CHP determined that a helicopter hoist offered the fastest and safest means of extricating the injured subject. The patient was subsequently evacuated by the helicopter and taken to Southern Inyo County Hospital.

ANALYSIS

The avalanche started in steep, northeast-facing terrain at around 10,800 feet, presumably as a loose snow slide. At around 10,400 feet, a large wet slab avalanche released on a deeper weak layer with an estimated two- to four-foot crown. The total slide length was about 2,500 feet. Rapidly warming temperatures, partly cloudy skies, and a weak overnight refreeze of the snowpack were all likely contributing factors. The nearest remote weather sensor (Charlotte Lake, 10,400 feet) recorded a low of 35°F at 4 a.m., rising to 56°F at 11 a.m.

The party estimated that ski penetration while they were skinning (mostly in the shady side of the chute) was no more than two inches, but on the sunny side it appeared to be softening more. They overestimated the surface refreeze, which they had felt was deeper. They both had transceivers on, but the rescue equipment in their packs was swept away by the slide, as they were in the middle of transitioning. The skiers had five and 12 years of backcountry experience, no formal avalanche education, but quite a bit of informal education from experienced partners.

With warm temperatures the snowpack is unstable, especially in the heat of the day. It is common practice among ski tourers to begin the day with an alpine start—getting up well before daylight and turning around as soon as the snow starts to soften. Both subjects are lucky to have survived this incident. (*Sources: Inyo County Search and Rescue and Eastern Sierra Avalanche Center.*)

LOWERING ERROR | Inexperience
Big Bear Lake Area, Holcomb Valley Pinnacles, Coyote Crag

On July 12, Ramiro Mosquera (24) was climbing with a group of friends on Bye Crackie (5.7), a 60-foot sport climb. After cleaning the anchor, Ramiro was being lowered when his belayer lost control of the brake strand threaded through a tube-style belay device. The belayer was unable to regain control, and Ramiro fell approximately 40 feet to the base of the route. He landed feet-first before falling onto his buttocks and back, with his head hitting the ground.

A passing climber identified herself as a physician and began stabilizing Ramiro's injuries. Two San Bernardino County Sheriff Department helicopters were dispatched to GPS coordinates provided by bystanders. After briefly landing to offload equipment and personnel to lighten the load, due to high summer temperatures and elevation (7,200 feet), Air Rescue 308 lowered a medic and a Stokes litter approximately 140 feet to the patient's location. After a hoist rescue, Ramiro was flown to Loma Linda University Medical Center trauma unit, where he was treated for an open left ankle pilon fracture, a right knee tibial plateau fracture, scalp laceration, and contusions.

ANALYSIS
As the most experienced member of a group enjoying a casual day at the crag, Ramiro felt that he had been a bit lax in reviewing and following safety protocols. Although they checked each other's harnesses and knots, Ramiro realizes that he did not adequately review his belayer's knowledge of techniques. With newer belayers, an additional climber can provide a backup by holding the brake strand behind the primary belayer. Properly used, assisted-braking devices also can offer an extra margin of safety when belaying and lowering.

No helmets were worn by anyone in the climbing party, and although Ramiro did not suffer any traumatic brain injury, his head wounds may have been lessened or prevented by a helmet. (*Sources: Ramiro Mosquera and San Bernardino County Sheriff-Coroner Department.*)

LOWERING ERROR | Complacency, No Stopper Knot
Joshua Tree National Park, Echo Rock, West Face

On February 8, our group of friends of varying abilities began climbing in the Echo Rock area of Joshua Tree. One of the climbers in our group was preparing to lead Touch and Go (5.9) and mentioned that an easier climb should be set up as a top-rope for those with less ability.

I (male, age 46) decided Double Dip (5.6) on Echo Rock would be good. I was arguably the most experienced in the group, with 22 years of on-and-off climbing. Several factors led to my incorrect determination that Double Dip was worthy of top-roping: I had done it several times (although many years ago); I felt a sense of urgency to set up a climb for the others; and I verified that we would be using a 70-meter rope, with the knowledge that a 60-meter wouldn't be long enough for a top-rope setup on this climb.

Rushing to rack up and tie in, I quickly chatted with my belayer, with whom I'd never climbed. I was confident that, if needed, I could comfortably solo Double Dip. My air of confidence seemed to silence any concerns my belayer may have had, and he deferred to my knowledge and experience.

At the top, I quickly set up an anchor at the bolted rappel station. Double Dip angles slightly to the right

A climber on Double Dip at Echo Rock. The top anchor is high and to the right of the climber. *Kailey Cox*

across the slab face of Echo Rock, and the fall line below the anchors lies along a 5.10 slab. While lowering, I spent my time admiring the 5.10, thinking it would be another enjoyable top-rope. At a point that people in my group estimated to be roughly 25 to 30 feet from the ground, the end of the rope slipped through my belayer's device and I began falling backward to the flat, sandy desert floor, at first backpedaling before skidding off the slab and landing on my shoulder and head.

ANALYSIS

After the accident, I was re-educated as to the length of the climb: 130 feet. Setting a top-rope required about 260 feet, and the 230-foot (70-meter) rope with stretch came up about 25 feet short.

There were several points at which the accident chain could have been broken. I could have asked the party that had just climbed Double Dip why they walked off; I could have tied a knot in the other end of the rope or had my belayer tie in; I could have asked my belayer to watch for the middle marker or to watch the rope as he lowered me; and, as an experienced climber, I certainly should have noted that I climbed more than 35 meters to the bolted anchor.

I hold my belayer faultless. For argument's sake, the only thing he could have done differently was watch for the end of the rope. However, considering the certainty in my actions, his deferral to my experience, and my emphasis that a 70-meter rope would reach, he had no reason to believe otherwise. Ultimately, I failed to follow some basic safety protocols. The jovial atmosphere and comfort of familiarity lulled me into a false sense of security.

After much speculation for the worst, my only injuries besides some scrapes and bruises were a fractured transverse process and a compression between C6 and C7 vertebra causing numbness down my left arm. The neck injury has since recovered with extensive physical therapy. Aside from sheer luck, I credit my survival to several factors: I landed on a flat sandy surface; I was wearing a helmet; the friction through the carabiners and drag over the slab helped reduce my rate of acceleration; a few in my group had medical training and certification and leapt into immediate action; and I was afforded the fantastic and professional response of JOSAR. (*Source: Anonymous Climber.*)

GROUND FALL | Protection Pulled Out
Joshua Tree National Park, Real Hidden Valley, Hidden Tower

On February 9, near the end of a good weekend of climbing, my partner/wife (female, 61) and I (male, 61) headed to Hidden Tower to climb Sail Away. A party of four was just starting that route, so instead we set up to climb Split, a 5.6 hand crack around the corner. [*The consensus rating at Mountain Project is 5.7+, and some consider this route to be even harder.*] I built a two-piece anchor for my wife at the belay, due to a small stance with a 15-foot drop onto rocks to the right of the belay pedestal.

The route starts with a short stretch of very low-angle rock before the crack rears up. I placed two cams (probably Camalots 1 and 2) in the crack and was above the second piece when I fell. Both cams pulled and I fell approximately 30 feet, past the belay. I don't remember feeling pumped or in any way having problems prior to the fall. My wife thinks she might have noted some type of rockfall, but was too traumatized by the circumstances to recall clearly.

I was helped by nearby climbers until JOSAR arrived and then packaged with spinal injury precautions and rolled in a litter to the Real Hidden Valley parking lot, and then taken by helicopter to a local hospital. I had multiple fractures and a collapsed right lung, but fortunately no spinal cord or head injuries. My right buttock was severely bruised—the Grigri and its locking carabiner that hung on my harness probably caused this. I have mostly recovered and was able to start climbing again by July 2020.

ANALYSIS
Things I think I did right were wearing a helmet (my wife too) and building a belay anchor for the exposed stance. I don't know why the cams pulled but believe the low-angle start of the route may have adversely affected the angle of placements on the

ESSENTIALS

WILDERNESS MEDICINE

By Seth C. Hawkins, MD, and Corey Winstead, WEMT

Anyone reading this book understands the value of wilderness medical training. Fortunately, climbers have numerous ways to obtain formal education. Wilderness medicine is now both an industry, with multiple private schools, as well as its own medical specialization. Concurrent with this growth is increased complexity for the consumer. This is an unregulated field (for the wilderness portions of the training), and there is no standard progression, so it's up to students to research the types and quality of training they seek. This article reviews some of the basic course types.

Wilderness First Aid (WFA) and its various iterations remain the standard for entry-level wilderness medicine training. WFA courses generally run from 8 to 24 hours, with most in the sweet spot of 16 hours—perfect for a long weekend. More advanced skills and information are offered in Advanced Wilderness First Aid classes (AWFA or WAFA), which run up to about 32 hours.

Wilderness First Responder (WFR) courses are generally recognized as the baseline for guides and highly motivated recreational climbers. These courses are about 80 hours. The non-regulated WFR credential is mostly used in private industry or for recreationalists, while the Wilderness Emergency Medical Responder (WEMR) credential is increasingly the standard for mountain rescue and search and rescue teams. WEMR courses are about 105 hours.

Those seeking more advanced training without prerequisites can obtain **Wilderness Emergency Medical Technician (WEMT)** certification. Like WEMR, this certification links wilderness modules (which are unregulated) with an EMT certification (which is state-regulated). WEMT courses run about 250 hours and include front-country in-field training elements such as ambulance ride-along time.

There also are environment-specialized classes, such as Vertical Medicine Resources (VMR)'s **Climber First Aid** classes or the National Ski Patrol's **Outdoor Emergency Care (OEC)** certification. First-aid classes such as VMR's generally require the same amount of time as a traditional class but have a focus on climbing, whereas OEC offers skills and training that exceed that of EMR but are not as extensive as EMT.

For those who already have a medical credential (paramedic, physician, nurse, etc.), further training opportunities abound. These include certification in **Advanced Wilderness Life Support** (AWLS), the **Wilderness Upgrade for Medical Professionals** (WUMP), **Fellowship in the Academy of Wilderness Medicine** (FAWM), and others.

Six prominent organizations in this field have formed the Wilderness Medicine Education Collaborative (Aerie Backcountry Medicine, Desert Mountain Medicine, NOLS Wilderness Medicine, Stonehearth Open Learning Opportunities (SOLO), Wilderness Medical Associates International, and the Wilderness Medicine Training Center International). These organizations have a track record of quality and recognize each other's credentials. Numerous other high-quality programs exist. Key elements to seek include instructor credentials, instructor field experience, hands-on components (always preferred!), and field applicability of the skills taught.

steeper crack. I have been trad leading for about five years and have taken a few falls on my gear without previous failures. I also have climbed with multiple AMGA guides and had some of them critique and approve my gear placements. (*Source: Neal Lischner.*)

Editor's Note: Both of these Joshua Tree rescues used the emergency phone at the Hidden Valley Campground/Intersection parking lot. Climbers should familiarize themselves with this location, as cell service is limited within the park.

STRANDINGS | Inadequate Protection, Inexperience
Tahquitz Rock

Riverside Mountain Rescue Unit (RMRU) performed multiple rescues on Lily Rock (a.k.a. Tahquitz Rock) during 2020. Two of the incidents involved climbers underestimating routes and calling for help when they became stranded.

On May 5, a leader ran out of protection while attempting to link pitches three and four of Whodunit (a.k.a. Hoodenett, 5.9). The leader felt that his last placement (a number 4 nut) was inadequate to protect a fall and did not feel that downclimbing was a viable option. Because the climbers were linking pitches with a 60-meter rope, they did not have enough available rope to lower the leader. The belayer was on a large ledge, but the leader was stuck on a small shelf protruding about four inches from the wall.

The pair activated 911 at about 6 p.m., and Riverside Sheriff Aviation Unit Star-9 helicoptered ropes and technical gear to the top of the route for members of the RMRU, who descended to the stranded climbers. Working throughout the night, RMRU assisted each climber down the cliff safely.

In the evening of December 5, RMRU responded to another pair of climbers who became stranded, reportedly after the lead climber had "run out of rope and protection" near the top of El Whampo (a five-pitch 5.7 route). An RMRU team was inserted at the top of the cliff by helicopter in a nighttime operation. The two climbers were located, uninjured but separated, with the leader about 150 feet below the end of the technical climbing and the second 150 feet farther down. A member of the team was lowered from the summit area to reach the leader, and both were hauled to the summit, and then the process was repeated with the second climber. After the climbers were rewarmed, they and the RMRU team members were flown from the summit. Everyone was back at the team's base by 3 a.m. (*Source: Riverside Mountain Rescue Unit.*)

ANALYSIS
Tahquitz (officially Lily Rock, according to the USGS) and neighboring Suicide Rock attract climbers of various levels. The ratings of these traditional routes are considered "old school," and many climbers have underestimated the difficulty of classic routes. Adequate research, planning, and protection are necessary before setting out, particularly when attempting a multi-pitch climb during the very short days of winter.

A generous rack and/or careful rationing of protection are necessary to safely link pitches on a sustained rock climb, or else the leader may run out of protection (or, more likely, the right sizes of protection). In the Whodunit incident, a rescuer who was carrying a complete rack was able to construct a solid anchor at the point where the leader had been stranded. (*Source: The Editors.*)

STRANDED | Avalanches
San Jacinto Mountain, North Face

On April 24, Riverside Mountain Rescue Unit (RMRU) received a call-out at 3:30 pm for two subjects who had been attempting the Snow Creek route on the north face of San Jacinto Peak. (This is one of the largest mountain escarpments in the Lower 48, rising more than 9,000 feet from the valley to the 10,839-foot summit.) Luckily, they had a cell signal and were able to report that they were okay but were stuck at about 7,000 feet, unable to move up or down due to extreme avalanche danger. It was over 100°F

Helicopter returns to base below the north face of San Jacinto Peak, which rises more than 9,000 feet above the desert floor. The Snow Creek route follows obvious gullies to the summit. *Blake Douglas*

on the desert floor, and a heavy snowstorm had occurred in early April.

Rescuers responded by helicopter, dropping two team members on a rock outcropping 50 yards below the subjects. This area was safely out of the couloir on climber's right. The climbers were a bit shaken up but uninjured. One of them was without a pack and reported that an avalanche had taken it.

The helicopter crew returned and performed a hover step, and one of the subjects and a rescuer climbed aboard. While the other two were waiting for the helicopter to return, they witnessed a loose wet slide in the adjacent gully bed that lasted over 90 seconds. (*A video of this avalanche can be seen at the* Accidents *website: publications. americanalpineclub.org.*) The helicopter soon returned and retrieved the remaining subject and rescuer.

ANALYSIS

The two had started at midnight from the utility station on the desert floor and made it to 7,000 feet by the afternoon, when large loose wet avalanches started occurring. They escaped the couloir by climbing onto a rocky outcropping, but not before one of them was struck by a large block of snow. He had lost the equipment he carried except for his helmet, which had a broken strap as a result of the impact. They considered descending, but the wet slides continued and they did not feel comfortable down-climbing the huge chockstone (3rd/4th class) at 5,500 feet. These two made the right choice to stay where they were and call for help.

Snow Creek is on the tick list for more and more people. When attempting a route like this, it is imperative to have more than physical fitness and route-finding skills. Understanding the snow conditions is crucial for safely completing this route. Conditions may be favorable for only a few years each decade, and for only a few weeks in those years. In this case, the heavy snowfall earlier in the month was poised to slide and funnel into this drainage in the spring heat.

It is also worth noting that, when traveling in high-risk mountain terrain, brightly colored clothing greatly helps with being spotted if a rescue is needed. It took a while to find the subjects since they were wearing all dark clothing and blended in with the rocks and terrain. (*Source: Tyler Shumway, Riverside Mountain Rescue Unit.*)

BELAY ERROR
El Cajon Mountain, Mountaineers Wall

On February 8, two seasoned climbers were planning to climb Sleeping Giant (5.10a), a ten-pitch mostly bolted climb. Finding the route already occupied with a party of five, with a single lead climber, AC (37) and his partner warmed up on nearby single-pitch routes. Once the longer route was sufficiently cleared, they climbed the first nine pitches without incident. Leading the 5.10a crux of the final pitch, AC took a fall approximately three feet above his last piece of protection. His belayer lost control of the brake strand through her tube-style device and AC fell 30 feet into a gully. He was wearing a helmet.

AC sustained a closed right bimalleolar ankle fracture. The party of five, who were rappelling nearby, witnessed the fall and called 911. AC was able to complete two rappels to the ground adjacent to the formation, and from there a CAL FIRE helicopter extricated him to a nearby ambulance.

ANALYSIS
It is unknown what caused the experienced belayer to lose control of the brake strand, although fatigue and distraction from the other climbers in the area may have been issues. AC also was out of sight of the belayer and fell unexpectedly. There were no burns on the belayer's hands. Any belayer can be affected by factors within and out of their control, and an assisted-braking device may reduce the chances of a significant fall and injury. (*Source: Andrew Camp.*)

HEAT STROKE
El Cajon Mountain

On August 22, two climbers completed Meteor (multi-pitch sport, 5.8) and multiple rappels to the base of the climb. After separating during the hike back to the car, Climber 2 realized his partner was delayed. He hiked back up and located Climber 1 on the trail, unresponsive. A satellite messenger was used to connect to emergency services, and Lakeside Fire personnel responded and transported Climber 1 to the hospital. There he was diagnosed with severe heat stroke, requiring life support and multiple organ transplants during his long road to recovery.

ANALYSIS
Climbing the main wall at El Cajon requires an arduous two-mile approach of 1,800 vertical feet. The hike and south-facing crag have little shade and can heat up quickly, particularly in the summer. These climbers took rest breaks and were prepared with plenty of water and a satellite messenger that allowed rapid rescue and medical treatment, which likely saved this climber's life. (*Sources: Instagram and GoFundMe posts.*)

ESSENTIALS

CLIMBING AND HEAT ILLNESS

By Christy Rosa Mohler, MD, FACEP

Climbers often consider hypothermia and frostbite as part of their risk assessment. Yet, heat-related illnesses can be a significant and often bigger threat in many regions. Heat illness is a preventable condition ranging in severity from mild heat cramps and heat edema to more serious heat exhaustion and life-threatening heat stroke. Certain medications, extremes of age (young and old), and pre-existing levels of fitness and/or medical conditions put certain populations at increased risk, but heat illness and exertional heat stroke can occur in otherwise healthy individuals as a result of strenuous activity in hot weather.

PREVENTION

Good planning before leaving home is the most important way to prevent heat illness. Avoid routes or approaches/descents in sun-exposed areas during high temperatures. Cooler temperatures are not without risk, as rocks hold and radiate heat, and exertion has an important role in heat illnesses. Prior to climbing in warmer areas, acclimatizing to heat over 10 to 14 days can reduce risk. During climbs, stay hydrated by "drinking to thirst" and wear loose-fitting clothing. Drinking excess water prior to climbing or "pre-cooling" are not effective for prevention.

SYMPTOMS

Initial complaints of thirst, muscle cramps, dizziness, weakness, nausea, and headache can progress quickly to vomiting, lethargy, slurred speech, agitation, seizures, and coma. Individuals may be sweating profusely or skin can be red and dry. Heart rate and respiratory rate are often rapid.

PREHOSPITAL MANAGEMENT

Early recognition and treatment of heat illness is crucial to outcome. The most important initial step is to remove the individual from the warm environment. If immediate extraction is not possible, move to any available shade. Placing an individual on a sleeping mat, backpack, or clothing can reduce heat transfer from the ground.

For mild illness in climbers with a normal level of consciousness, treatment can be as simple as cessation of physical activity and rehydration with fluids (water or electrolyte drinks) in a cooler environment. Because there is often an overlap between heat illness and low sodium levels, salty foods or fluids can also be considered.

More severe illness, such as heat exhaustion or heat stroke (defined as core temperature above 104°F with changes in mental status), require rapid evacuation for medical treatment, with more aggressive cooling measures started immediately and continuing during transport. Active cooling measures–from most to least effective–include immersion in ice water or a natural body of water, wetting the victim with tepid water and then fanning them, and ice packs placed on the groin, neck, and in the armpits.

Unless symptoms are mild and completely resolve in a short time, all patients should be rapidly transported for medical assessment and care.

COLORADO

AVALANCHE ONTO ICE CLIMBER | Terrain Trap
Ouray Area, Uncompahgre Gorge

Around 8 a.m. on January 18, a guide and three clients departed Ouray for ice climbing in the Uncompahgre Gorge. From U.S. Highway 550, the group descended a snowy slope, crossed Red Mountain Creek, and ascended another slope to the base of a climbing area known as the Dungeon or Petefish Slabs.

The guide led a pitch and set up a top-rope for the clients. Climbers 1 and 2 climbed the route with no issues and lowered to the base. While Climber 3 ascended the route, Climber 1 moved slightly to the north of the route to take pictures while Climber 2 remained south of the guide, who belayed from under the route. Suddenly, the group heard a loud cracking noise and ice and snow rained down. Climber 3 (on the route) was hit by several chucks of ice but was not injured. Once the air cleared, the group realized the snow and ice had hit and buried Climber 1.

The guide lowered Climber 3, who called 911. The guide and Climber 2 immediately descended the slope and searched for Climber 1 by digging through the debris with their hands. They couldn't find Climber 1 and thought they may have been buried in Red Mountain Creek. However, the climbers could not search the creek bottom because of a fragile snow and ice bridge and fast-flowing water underneath. The guide and Climber 2 ascended back to the belay ledge, where there was cell phone service, and the guide activated SOS via inReach and placed additional phone calls informing authorities of the exact location and situation.

At 11:38 a.m., Ouray Mountain Rescue (OMR) arrived at milemarker 89 and descended the snowy slope. They immediately began probing, which initially

The Dungeon, near Ouray. (A) Ice pillar that broke and triggered an avalanche. (B) Location of belayer and Climber 2. (C) Location of Climber 1. The avalanche carried Climber 1 down to Red Mountain Creek (off-photo) and buried the climber. *CAIC Photo*

produced several false-positive strikes. A rescue team member broke through t bridge, revealing the flowing water of the creek. At 12:23 p.m., a rescue team me found Climber 1 with a probe strike. The avalanche had buried Climber 1 head-down in the creek bed under approximately five feet of ice and snow. Resuscitation efforts from a paramedic were unsuccessful.

ANALYSIS

January 18 had dawned clear and cold after a two-day storm ended the night before. A weather station one mile south of the accident site measured three inches of new snow in the previous 24 hours. The weather station recorded a low temperature of 0°F at 4 a.m., and the temperature rose to 10°F by 10 a.m.

In most avalanche accidents, the person injured by the avalanche or someone in that person's party triggers the slide. (In Colorado over the last 30 years, only about seven percent of fatal avalanche accidents have involved a natural or spontaneous avalanche.) In this accident, however, a large chunk of ice broke away from a supported pillar and triggered a small loose snow avalanche (approximately four inches deep) on the rock slab below.

The mix of broken ice and snow debris flowed over an ice-covered cliff and entrained additional loose snow on the slope below before stopping in the creek. The moving snow alone was not enough to injure or bury a person, but the large chunks of ice striking the victim and/or burial in the terrain trap below produced a fatal outcome.

This is the fifth fatal avalanche accident in Colorado during the past 10 years that involved a climber (about seven percent of avalanche fatalities over that 10-year period). None of the climbers in the group was carrying avalanche rescue equipment, such as shovels and probes. Although it is not uncommon for ice climbers to venture into the mountains without this gear, it does limit their options in the event of an avalanche accident. In this case, the group's initial rescue effort was limited to digging with their hands and ice tools in probable locations. Technical climbers should consider carrying avalanche rescue equipment, though in this case, given the nature of the debris and the narrow gorge below, it is unlikely the outcome would have been different. (*Source: Colorado Avalanche Information Center.*)

LONG LEADER FALL | Protection Pulled Out
Black Canyon of the Gunnison National Park, North Chasm Wall

On the morning of June 2, a party of four descended the Cruise Gully to attempt Scenic Cruise, a 13-pitch 5.10d trad route on the North Chasm Wall. The group planned to climb as two parties of two. While leading pitch five, a long 5.10 finger and hand crack, one of the climbers fell about 50 feet, as two pieces of protection pulled out of the crack. The climber suspected a broken ankle, and both parties initiated self-rescue to the base of the climb.

Around 1 p.m., one of the climbers from the injured party began to ascend the Cruise Gully to get help, and he happened to run into a climbing ranger conducting routine work in the gully. The ranger climbed to the North Rim to retrieve first-aid equipment and establish communications channels, and then returned to meet the climbers at the bottom of the canyon.

With the injured climber stranded in the canyon at the base of the climb, there were two rescue options: a 1,600-foot rope raise of the injured climber by the Black Canyon of the Gunnison volunteer SAR team or a short-haul helicopter rescue by Mesa Verde Helitack. After confirming their availability, Mesa Verde Helitack arrived on scene and conducted a reconnaissance flight around 4:30 p.m. The ranger and the three remaining climbers carried the injured climber to an opening in the center of the gully. After reconfiguring at the South Rim's helipad, Mesa Verde's Bell 407 and short-haul spotter and attendant successfully lifted the injured climber to the North Rim for the first-ever short-haul rescue in Black Canyon of the Gunnison National Park.

The first-ever short-haul helicopter rescue from the base of the Black Canyon. Because of limited helicopter availability and difficult conditions, climbers cannot count on a speedy short-haul rescue from this deep canyon. *NPS Photo*

ANALYSIS

The Black Canyon is known for extreme temperature swings and can be very hot in midsummer. Early June was warmer than the seasonal norms in 2020, and the Scenic Cruise route is in full sun. It's certainly possible the difficult conditions and/or haste contributed to the leader's fall and to inadequate placements on this sustained but well-protected pitch.

Over the last few seasons, more parties have been climbing in bigger groups in the Black, which is not recommended. There is an abundance of loose rock on these walls, even on the trade routes, and the likelihood of parties below being hit by rockfall is significant.

Luckily, there was enough rope for the belayer to lower the injured climber to the belay, and then the second pair's rope expedited self-rescue. Many pitches in the Black Canyon are 50 to 60 meters long, and climbers should be prepared to handle scenarios that would not allow lowering of the leader.

Due to the technical terrain and remoteness of the inner Black Canyon, rescue response times can be elongated by several hours or into the next day. The only escape to the rim from the bottom in this area is the Cruise Gully, which involves 5.7 climbing (there are two fixed rappels for the descent). If a party is unable to ascend this route, the only rescue options are a rope raise (which usually must take place the following day) or a helicopter. While the new short-haul helicopter program is a great resource, Mesa Verde Helitack may be on other assignments or the weather and conditions may not allow for a short-haul rescue.

In summary, it is not easy to get out of the canyon if injured. Black Canyon climbers need to come prepared and approach routes with a conservative mentality. (*Source: Tom Schaefer, ranger, Black Canyon of the Gunnison National Park.*)

ROCKFALL ONTO BELAYER
Rifle Mountain Park, Ruckman Cave

At approximately 4 p.m. on September 26, a climber started up The Promise, a 5.12c sport route on the left side of the Ruckman Cave. Just before a ledge at the start of the steep climbing on the route, the climber pulled onto a chalked-up jug that ripped out of the wall. The broken jug, along with more rocks and debris, rained down on the belayer. The climber's fall was held at the first bolt of the route, and he slammed into the wall sideways, from which he sustained soreness and bruising. The belayer narrowly avoided being hit in the head or upper body by the debris and took all of the damage to his right leg. Fortunately, a visit to the emergency department confirmed no broken bones. (*Source: Climber's report at MountainProject.com.*)

ANALYSIS
This incident highlights a paradox often seen at sport climbing areas: The climbers who choose to wear helmets while sport climbing more often are the ones leading or top-roping the climb, not necessarily the belayers and bystanders below the route. Yet, arguably, the belayer is much more likely to be hit by rockfall, which is fairly common on Rifle Mountain Park's limestone.

More common than helmets at Rifle's crags are assisted-braking belay devices, which can be a lifesaver in accidents like this one, when the belayer may be severely distracted or even incapacitated by rockfall. (*Source: The Editors.*)

GROUND FALL | Failure to Clip Bolt
Shelf Road, Cactus Cliff

In September, during a weekend trip to Shelf Road, my wife took a ground fall while leading Ian's Climb (5.7+) at Cactus Cliff. She couldn't clip the second bolt, fell and hit the ground, tripped backward, and hit her head. She was wearing a helmet. She was dazed and after a few minutes started to complain of memory loss; she didn't know where she was or what had happened. Nearby climbers with medical training checked her out and said there was a hematoma on the back of her head; one of them who was a nurse urged me to get her to medical attention soon so internal bleeding could be ruled out. We left our draws on the route, asking other climbers to retrieve them for us, and walked back to the parking lot, from which I drove her to the hospital for a CT scan.

ANALYSIS
My wife decided to lead the route even though she wasn't feeling super psyched about it. I had grunted and hollered a bit as I led it, and that might have made her a bit nervous. She wanted to top-rope, but the rope's fall line went straight down a 5.10c because I had left no directionals. She then said, "I'll just lead it." The route's description says the crux is at the second bolt, with some bouldery moves, and that's where she missed her clip. Later, my wife and I agreed that, since she was not feeling confident about the climb, she could have downclimbed a bit and lowered off. [*Editor's Note: Nervous leaders also can consider stick-clipping the second bolt of*

a sport climb, which substantially improves the odds against a ground fall in case of a slip above the first bolt.]

I screwed up in my position as the lead belayer, standing down on the ground instead of up on a higher ledge directly below the route. My belay position lengthened the amount of rope in the system, and she continued to stumble backward even as her feet hit the ground. I was trying to move closer to that ledge, taking up slack as I did, when my wife went for the clip.

We're so glad she was wearing a helmet, without which she might have suffered a worse head injury. (*Source: Samir Chopra.*)

FATAL FALL IN SANGRE DE CRISTO RANGE: *On October 10, a climber disappeared after summiting Ellingwood Point (14,042 feet). After a five-day search, she was discovered to have fallen to her death while descending a 3rd-class route. The full report from Alamosa Volunteer Search and Rescue is at publications.americanalpineclub.org.*

FALL ON ROCK | Climbing Unroped
Longs Peak, North Chimney

On September 5, I planned to climb D7 (5.11c) on the Diamond of Longs Peak, approaching via the North Chimney. This is the most common approach to the Diamond and is a 500-foot rock climb rated 5.4. My partner and I had started up the trail at 7 a.m., arriving at the base of the North Chimney around 9:30 a.m. We were with two friends who would be roping up at the base of the North Chimney just below us. My climbing partner and I had soloed the North Chimney together earlier in the summer, so we didn't discuss if we were comfortable with this—it was implied. Additionally, with our relatively late start time, there was nobody on the route above us, which was positive, considering the high risk of rockfall on this route.

As we began ascending the North Chimney, my partner stopped after about 100 feet to switch into climbing shoes. I was wearing my approach shoes, and I felt comfortable continuing in them, as I frequently climb low 5th class in them and had already done this approach in them twice before. As we climbed, my partner was moving faster than me and stayed 10 to 30 feet in front. I noticed that we were going a different way than I usually go. I didn't worry about it, because my partner is a strong and experienced climber and I generally trust his route-finding skills. About 200 feet up, I suddenly realized I was kind of stuck. Backing off seemed very tenuous. My climbing partner was out of sight, maybe 30 feet ahead of me. I thought about mentioning my predicament, but it felt overly dramatic. After about a minute, I decided that I could not stay in the position I was in much longer.

I do not remember if I committed to backing off or going forward, but I slipped off. I tumbled to climber's right onto some snow. As recounted by my climbing partners after the incident, I alternated between sliding on my front and back as I fell down the snow, but stayed head up. There was a break in the snow about 30 feet above the mouth of the North Chimney that likely slowed my fall. I continued to slide down the snow below the chimney and stopped in the talus field below. I don't recall the exact details of the fall, but my helmet had a crack in the back.

The friends below us were first to get to me. One of them is an EMT and was my primary rescuer until the RMNP ranger team arrived and prepared me for a helicopter flight to the hospital. I suffered two fractured front ribs (right side), a small closed pneumothorax (right side), a 20 percent compression T6 back fracture, seven stitches to repair a bone-deep laceration to my left eyebrow, sprained right ankle, bone-bruised/sprained (unknown) left foot, and a multitude of abrasions on my chin, arms, back and chest. Additionally, I likely had a mild concussion.

ANALYSIS

Accidents usually involve bad luck, but sometimes they also reflect the absence of good luck—as in when you are doing something incorrect or sloppy and don't get away with it. In my case, I think both situations apply. Alpine climbing and scrambling have inherent risk, and bad things can happen even if you do everything right.

The Diamond on Longs Peak. (A) Approximate location of fatal fall from Broadway ledge in the incident described below. (B) Approximate location of fall from the North Chimney approach to the face. The ledges had less snow at the time of these accidents. *Stefan and Richard Hollos*

Because we both felt comfortable on the terrain, the choice between roping up and soloing the North Chimney felt obvious to me; the North Chimney is notorious for rockfall, and roping up increases the chances of knocking off loose rock. Soloing is also significantly faster, which means less exposure time in the rockfall zone. On the other hand, as I demonstrated, the consequences of soloing are very high.

I didn't know the route as well as I thought I did. Though this approach route may be 5.4—well within my ability level, even in approach shoes—15 feet away from the best line could be much harder. I wasn't paying much attention to the exact route we followed because my climbing partner was more experienced than me, we climb together frequently, and I assumed he would pick the path of least resistance. I also felt a competitive need to keep up with his pace. Expert halo, ego, and lack of attention are three serious human factors highlighted here. (*Source: Annie Weinmann.*)

FATAL FALL DURING APPROACH | Climbing Unroped
Rocky Mountain National Park, Longs Peak

On July 30, Dillon Blanksma, 26, fell from Broadway ledge during the approach to the Diamond wall. The fall was fatal. Blanksma and his climbing partner had done the standard North Chimney approach and were on their way to a route on the left side of the Diamond. Broadway is normally traversed by walking unroped, but toward its left side the ledge system narrows and slopes more steeply toward the 600- to 800-foot-high Lower East Face. To reach the start of climbs on this side, a band of fourth-class rock approximately 30 feet high must be climbed. Blanksma, still unroped, is believed to have fallen from on or near this section, possibly as a result of a loose hold. Dillon was a staff member at the American Alpine Club's Golden, Colorado, headquarters and is much missed by his colleagues, friends, and family.

ANALYSIS

At least four climbers have died in falls from Broadway. Three of them—including one in 2000 and another in 2010—were doing similar unroped approaches up fourth-class rock to reach their intended climbs. Although the granite on the Diamond face is generally very solid, Broadway and the short fourth-class band above the ledge are comprised of weathered alpine rock, with many potentially loose holds. Climbers are understandably in a hurry to reach their objectives on a busy wall that is prone to afternoon thunderstorms, but the history of accidents in this area suggests that roping up and belaying the final fourth-class approach would save lives. (*Source: The Editors.*)

FATAL FALL ABOVE GLACIER GORGE: *On September 10, Steven Grunwald, 24, was reported missing by a friend. His car was found parked in the Glacier Gorge parking lot in Rocky Mountain National Park the same day. Grunwald was last seen on August 28 and his exact plans were unknown, but he was thought to be attempting the Glacier Gorge Traverse, a 19-mile route that includes multiple technical summits up to 5.7. After an extensive ground and aerial search, his body was found at the top of the McHenry's Notch Couloir, between McHenry's and Powell peaks, on September 14. Grunwald is believed to have died from a fall, though the cause is unknown. This incident is a reminder of the vital importance of telling someone your plans or itinerary before a solo trip into the mountains, which can greatly speed a rescue or ease the burden of searchers in case something goes wrong.*

The scene after a long fall from the Juliet Couloir, the snow chute in upper left. The climber had nearly reached the cornice at the top before falling. *Rocky Mountain Rescue Group*

FALL ON SNOW | Failure to Self-Arrest
Indian Peaks Wilderness, Mt. Neva, Juliet Couloir

At 5:30 a.m. on June 11, a 22-year-old male left the Fourth of July trailhead to attempt the Juliet Couloir, a short, moderate snow route on Mt. Neva (12,814 feet). As he was nearing the cornice at the top, he fell. He had an ice axe but failed to self-arrest. The climber fell the length of the couloir, hitting some rocks on the way down and sustaining multiple injuries, including a fractured femur. He activated his Garmin inReach just after 8 a.m. and was able to transmit his location and condition to rescuers. He was extracted by helicopter hoist and transferred to a ground ambulance.

ANALYSIS

The ability to self-arrest on steep, soft snow is a prerequisite for spring and summer snow climbs. Repeated practice will improve one's chances of stopping a slide.

The climber's use of a satellite communication device was invaluable in transmitting timely, accurate information, including GPS coordinates of his exact location. This was essential to organizing the right resources for his rescue, which involved the Colorado Hoist Rescue Team; the CHRT is a collaboration between military aviation assets from Buckley Air Force Base and civilian SAR personnel from Rocky Mountain Rescue Group. (*Sources: Rocky Mountain Rescue Group and the Editors.*)

GROUND FALL | Inadequate Protection
Boulder Canyon, Castle Rock

In the evening of October 1, professional climber Molly Mitchell (27) attempted a traditionally protected ascent of Crank It (5.13c/d, a.k.a. Slabio) at the base of Castle Rock. The route is bolted, and she had climbed it previously using the bolts; now her goal was to lead the route while placing her own protection. The route has two separate cracks, one to the left down low, and then a crux section of face climbing to reach the next crack up and to the right. The climb follows this crack to the anchor around 40 feet up. Previously, in 2016, Brad Gobright fell from about 15 to 18 feet up while trying to lead this route on gear, and he ripped the one piece he had placed and decked. He broke his back and ankle.

Molly got through the crux and fell after her foot slipped about 25 to 30 feet up. The fall ripped out four of the pieces of gear she placed, and she decked. (The gear that pulled out of the crack–from top to bottom–included a small RP nut, a purple Totem Cam, a small offset nut, and a medium-size nut.) Fortunately, she landed on a bouldering pad that she and her partner had laid out for the lower section, just in case. Nonetheless, she ended up with compression fractures in her L2 and L3 vertebrae. No surgery was needed because nothing was displaced, but she had to wear a back brace for nine weeks.

ANALYSIS
After thinking about this a lot and watching the video of the attempt (which will eventually be released), I believe that even though I had tested some of the pieces of gear before, by falling onto the gear with the bolts clipped as backup, the rope was running in a different spot during my trad attempt. The pro was in two separate cracks and the rope was not in a straight line. So that was one factor.

Also, the crack is very polished, shallow, and flaring. The pieces are incredibly specific, and sometimes even when they look OK, they will not hold a dynamic fall. The bottom piece that pulled out (the medium nut) was a solid piece of gear, but what happened–and what you will eventually see in the video–is the tension in the rope from ripping the upper pieces actually lifted this nut up and out of the crack. Had that nut held, I would not have hit the ground.

I want to emphasize that my belayer, Tanner, did an absolutely amazing job at trying to take in slack and move backward. There was nothing more he could have done to help the situation. It was a bad fall, and I take full responsibility for putting myself in that position.

I believed I had taken my time while rehearsing for this attempt and tried to figure out the gear. I had had a near-decking incident at the same spot a week prior, on gear

Molly Mitchell attempting Crank It with traditional protection. The four pieces that pulled out in her fall are marked. The lowest of these was a good nut, but the action of the rope during the fall apparently levered it out. *Tory Powers*

that I had tested yet still ripped, and this made me fully reanalyze my gear for that section. I thought it was better, but obviously I did not account for the rope position, the nut lifting out, and the fact that if you don't place those pieces perfectly on the go, they will not hold—slippery, cryptic granite! I think potentially a double rope system, anchoring down the lower nut so it wouldn't get pulled out, and making sure to really place each piece perfectly would have helped.

During my attempt, I was way more pumped than I had been while rehearsing in the middle section. I felt like I was not going to send, but didn't want to give up. My foot slipped on the next sequence. I definitely would have been better off clipping a bolt and calling it a day. But this is the fine line you walk in this territory of climbing—do you go for it or do you bail? Had I known the gear would rip, obviously I would have bailed. But hindsight is 20/20. (*Source: Molly Mitchell.*)

GROUND FALL | Protection Pulled Out
Boulder Canyon, Bell Buttress

On August 13, after climbing a few routes at Bell Buttress, I decided to give a redpoint attempt at Arms Bazaar (5.12a trad). I had spent two previous sessions on the route: one in August 2019 and one the previous week. I had the route fairly dialed and felt confident I could send it that day.

I racked all my gear in the order I intended to place it and began climbing. After clipping the lone bolt on the route, I did a few balancey moves to a good stance. From here, I placed a red Metolius cam in a horizontal crack with the stem facing downward. I clipped into this with a shoulder-length sling. This is a shallow crack, with the head of the cam just fitting in; the fit was tight and the lobes all had great contact, though, so I was not worried about the placement.

After a rest, I did a short traverse into the crux. From an undercling, I placed a black Metolius cam (approximately 1.25 inches) in the crack above me. Although the crack flares slightly, the black Metolius fits here decently well, and I had fallen on it multiple times. After placing this cam, I began the crux sequence. I fell with my waist at about the height of the top cam. Both of the cams I placed blew out, and I hit the ground from an estimated 25 feet high. I believe the bolt may have begun to catch me slightly as I hit the ground, although I am not sure.

My left side took pretty much all of the damage. About 20 to 30 seconds after the fall, I began to evaluate my condition with my partner. We confirmed that I was not bleeding or deformed anywhere (especially on my skull), so I sat down and just began to think and chat with my partner in order to determine my mental state, which was normal, considering the circumstances. I ended up with a bruised left hip, bruised left heel, and a sore thumb. The foam on the right side of my helmet was completely cracked. I likely had a mild concussion, but I did not show any symptoms besides slight confusion for a minute or so after I fell.

ANALYSIS

First of all, I consider myself extremely lucky to have walked away from this fall with such minimal damage. If circumstances were just slightly different, my injuries would have been much more severe.

The protection pulling out was very surprising. I had fallen on the same black Metolius placement multiple times, during both prior attempts, and I also considered the red Metolius to be solid, albeit not perfect. The only explanation I can come up with is that the two pieces interacted with each other and the rope in such a way that they helped to torque each other out. The red Metolius was clipped with a shoulder-length sling, and this directed the rope at an estimated 45° angle down and left of the black Metolius placement.

It is worth noting that there is another possible placement (0.4 size) about eight inches under the black Metolius. I had placed a yellow Totem Cam here on some previous burns, but ultimately determined it was unnecessary. Had I placed this piece before I fell, I likely would not have decked. (I did take a few falls earlier onto the black Metolius *without* the yellow Totem Cam placed, so the Totem was not a necessity in preventing a funky interaction between the two Metolius cams.) Although the interaction between pieces when loaded can be difficult to predict, it's something trad climbers should give a lot of thought to, especially when redpointing, where one has time on the ground or while hangdogging to really analyze each placement and the system of protection as a whole.

Had I not been wearing a helmet, I believe I could have been very seriously injured. When trad climbing, everything gets harder to predict and control for, and the helmet is such an easy precaution to take. (*Source: Joel May, adapted from a post at Mountain Project, with permission.*)

FALL ON ROCK | Inadequate Protection
Boulder, First Flatiron

The 10-pitch, 1,000-foot east face of the First Flatiron, rated 5.6 R, was my goal for August 10. I had not put boot to rock in over six months, owing in part to inactivity compelled by the COVID-19 pandemic. My partner, age 56, and I (69) both began the route fresh off the couch, though we each have long trad climbing histories and much experience on routes far harder than this day's objective.

Starting the second pitch, the route looked unclear to us. I climbed straight up from our belay stance, following a few chalk marks, and placed two good pieces in the first 40 feet. A small, shallow pocket accepted a pink Tricam for my highest piece. I placed it carefully and it looked good. I pulled hard on the piece and it flew out easily.

The accident sites on (A) Second Flatiron (see next page) and (B) First Flatiron (this page). Located directly above Boulder, the east faces of these formations are hundreds of feet high.

This was disconcerting, but I replaced the Tricam, gave a gentle tug, and hoped for the best. The prospect of positive holds loomed 50 feet higher. Just before reaching them, I placed a small DMM nut.

Tired from the tension of this long, dicey lead, I thought exultantly, "I've got it in the bag." I transferred my weight onto a right foot hold, and my foot slipped unexpectedly. My first thoughts on the less-than-vertical face were to keep my feet under me and run down the face, waiting to be held by my protection. Quickly, gravity's acceleration exceeded my running ability and I tumbled, completely out of control. I came to a stop when I hit the belay ledge after several bounces, landing on my back. The rope was slack above me, having "caught my fall" only enough to rip out my top two pieces of protection. My top piece somehow came unclipped from the rope during my fall and was located by a party who followed us up the climb—it had landed nearly as high and 30 feet to the left of its original placement.

My partner and I devised a plan to rappel down a single line from the first anchor to the ground. Meanwhile, the climber who had been following us up the climb informed me I had drifted off route and taken a more difficult, direct alternative. Once we both were down on the ground, he untied our rope and we were off the face with all of our gear.

I slowly limped one mile back to the car and opted for first aid at my partner's home over a trip to the emergency room. My most debilitating injury was an extremely painful left shoulder, though the joint still had full range of motion. I also had abrasions on the left leg, a seriously bruised right big toe, a sprained right thumb, and gouges on the top of three fingers of the right hand. My back was spared injury because I'd been wearing a pack containing a half-empty water bottle that exploded on impact. No head or neck injury. I was very lucky.

ANALYSIS

To catalogue my errors:

- Too hard of an objective for an out-of-shape climber
- Too much pride to turn around when the objective proved tougher than expected

- Too much reliance on questionable gear
- And the one I really don't want to admit: I need to make concessions to the reality of growing old.

It's often said, "I'd rather be lucky than good." Only luck kept me from paying the ultimate price for my hubris. (*Source: Terry Price.*)

FATAL FALL ON ROCK | Climbing Without a Rope
Boulder, Second Flatiron

On October 30, 49-year-old Andrew Caplan fell from the north side of the Second Flatiron near the top of a climb. Boulder Open Space and Mountain Parks rangers arrived on scene just after 9:20 a.m. and began resuscitation efforts, but the patient did not survive.

ANALYSIS
GPS tracking from Strava suggests that Caplan hiked from the Chautauqua trailhead to the base of the Second Flatiron to climb Freeway (5.0), though his exact climbing route isn't known. This is a popular route for scrambling (free soloing) and is a route that Caplan was reported to have climbed "hundreds of times." The location where his body was discovered on a nearby trail suggests he fell during an exposed, low fifth-class section near the end of the route and then slid some distance. The area had received about a foot of snow in an early-season storm four days earlier. It was not clear if lingering snow or wet conditions contributed to Caplan's fall. (*Source: The Editors.*)

FALL ON ROCK | Fixed Protection Pulled Out
Boulder, Flatirons, Seal Rock

I have been frequenting the Flatirons for climbing since moving to Boulder five years ago. In the fall of 2020, I started projecting Primate, a 5.13b route at Seal Rock with a mix of bolt and traditional protection. I visited the route four times and climbed it about three times per session. I was very close to sending, and on November 8, I paired up with a friend who was visiting from out of town—she was up for trying the same route.

The route begins with easier climbing that I used to warm up, as the crag has few moderates. I began the initial 5.11 section, clipping a bolt and then a fixed nut. Once my feet were level with the fixed nut, one foot unexpectedly slipped, causing a barn-door motion that led to a fall. The nut held for an instant and then ripped out of the rock. I fell about 20 feet and landed on my back, directly on the belayer's rope stack. I was unable to breathe for about one minute, but then was able to stand up and eventually walk back to the car with my partner. I had narrowly avoided landing on a pointed rock next to the belay. A visit to urgent care confirmed I had luckily avoided any serious injury.

ANALYSIS
I did not properly assess the security of the fixed nut on this route. I had seen a

dozen others climb the route and clip this gear without inspection, and therefore I assumed it was trustworthy. The rock in this section is very friable, and I believe this contributed both to my foot slipping and to the gear pulling out.

Since this incident, I have been assessing fixed gear more thoroughly. I have discovered open quick links on fixed quickdraws and fixed draws with decade-old nylon slings, and I've had a hanger detach from a bolt while climbing. I hope others will be more careful in assessing the condition of fixed gear on their climbs, even if they have done a route a dozen times. (*Source: Patrick Hardy.*)

STRANDED | Unable to Find Descent Route
Eldorado Canyon State Park, Redgarden Wall

On March 22, two climbers called for assistance after dark when they were unable to find the descent route upon completing Anthill Direct (5 pitches, 5.9-). After searching for the correct way down in the dark without headlamps, and eventually getting their rope stuck on a rappel, they called for help. Rescuers climbed to them at night, in snowy conditions, and then guided them down the standard East Slabs descent (4th class). The rescue took approximately eight hours.

ANALYSIS
This pair started the route at 1:30 p.m. in March and finished in the dark. (Sunset on that date was at 7:15 p.m.) The East Slabs descent from Redgarden Wall is exposed and can be difficult to navigate for the first time even in daylight. Researching the descent as thoroughly as the ascent reduces the chances of a stranding like this.

One of the climbers involved in this incident had much less experience in multi-pitch climbing than her partner and deferred to him, even though she had concerns about the late start and their lack of knowledge about the descent. She encourages climbers to speak up and voice concerns to their partner and not to be intimidated or silenced by a gap in experience. (*Source: Rocky Mountain Rescue Group.*)

FALL ON ROCK | Protection Pulled Out
Eldorado Canyon State Park, West Ridge

On September 27, a climber fell to the ground while leading Funeral March (5.9+), a wide crack climb. Funeral March is protected by very large cams, and the climber bumped one of these up the crack for about 10 feet. He had placed another cam but had not yet clipped it when he fell, and the first piece pulled out. The climber had a number of injuries, including a concussion; he believes his helmet prevented a worse head injury.

ANALYSIS
It is not certain why the protection pulled out. When using large cams to protect offwidth routes, accidentally stepping on or kicking placed cams, rotational forces causing a cam to "walk" into a worse placement, and the tendency to place less protection or the wrong size ("tipped out") cams—often because of a shortage of large pieces—all may contribute to higher risk in the case of a leader fall. (*Sources: Climber post at Mountain Project and Rocky Mountain Rescue Group.*)

LOWERING ERROR | Distraction, No Stopper Knot
Clear Creek Canyon, Little Eiger

On August 10, I got off work at 5 p.m. and my partner and I set out to Little Eiger, a crag we had never visited. I knew from reading some route descriptions that we would need a 70-meter rope and at least 16 draws. We first climbed Busch Gardens (5.10), directly above the approach trail, and I took a few falls near the top. It was obvious that I was tired from work, which I feel contributed to what happened next.

My partner top-roped Busch Gardens and I belayed. We had forgotten the rope bag, which I use as a safety tool; I always tie a triple barrel knot and then overhand it around the red marker on the rope tarp. This was the first deviation from our normal practice.

We finished up Busch Gardens and moved onto Is Our Children Learning? (5.9+) at the far right end of the crag. I coiled the rope directly into my pack and did not tie a stopper knot, though I didn't think about it at the time.

The route starts with a large overhang protected by a bolt, leaning out over a small, eroding landing zone, which sits above a steep, rocky hillside that falls to the road about 80 feet below. As I belayed my partner's lead climb, I noticed the middle mark on the rope pass through my Grigri, but it did not pass the first bolt before she reached the anchor so I didn't think too much about it. My partner was planning to clean the draws off the route, which I figured would allow for enough extra rope to safely lower her.

Given the arching nature of the route, cleaning the pitch was more difficult than normal and I was distracted with trying to help her. When she was about four feet above the ground, I heard the horrific sound of the rope snapping through the Grigri. I tried to grab for the rope, which sent me tumbling after her down the steep hillside. We rolled about 40 feet and came to a stop on a tiny shrub. I am sure going the rest of the way would have resulted in a much worse outcome. We were extremely lucky and were left with bad bruises and some good cuts, but nothing major.

ANALYSIS

Tying a knot and closing the system would have prevented this entire scenario. In my studies of avalanche accidents, the human factor is something all the experts talk about. This was not a breakdown of knowledge or systems—this was human error. Was it simple complacency? Was it a lack of focus? Stupidity, fatigue, arrogance? Most likely all of these and yet none of them. The best single explanation I have come to is that we failed to follow through our system/safety checks 100 percent. My takeaway for the future—and the takeaway I hope to convey to the community—is to never skip a full safety check before every route. (*Source: Anonymous climber.*)

EDITOR'S NOTE: *This route and others at this crag require a full 70-meter rope to lower safely. Although it was not a critical issue in this incident, dynamic ropes often vary from their stated length, and with age they can shrink by up to 10 percent of their initial length (that's more than 22 feet on a 70-meter rope). Moreover, according to Petzl, ropes may shrink unevenly, meaning a middle marker may become inaccurate over time. All of which reinforces the climber's main point: Close the system and do a full safety review with your partner—harness, tie-in, stopper knot, belay set-up, and a plan for cleaning the anchor—before every climb.*

Jackson's Thumb showing the location of the two rappel anchors (X) and the spot where a climber accidentally rappelled too far and fell (arrow). After her injury, other climbers helped her continue the rappel into the gully at right. *Stephen King*

IDAHO

RAPPEL ERROR | Off Route
City of Rocks National Reserve

In the midafternoon of May 31, rangers at the City of Rocks National Reserve received word that a 67-year-old female climber had fallen while rappelling from Jackson's Thumb and had reportedly broken her ankles. She and her partner had ascended Theater of Shadows (5.6), a four-pitch, 400-foot bolted climb, and while rappelling from the top, she descended below the second rappel station and into a cleft between the Thumb formation and an adjoining wall.

Upon realizing her mistake, she began to climb back up to the second rappel station to regain the normal rappel line. While ascending, she neglected to pull the accumulating slack through her rappel device. At some point she slipped and fell 15 to 20 feet, striking her feet against the wall and injuring her ankles. The climber was able to arrest her fall and maintain her position while her partner rappelled to the ground along with two climbers from another party, who then provided a fireman's belay to assist her down a lower-angle slab to the base of the face.

At 3:42 p.m., rangers Ryan Buffington and Savana Jones made contact with the injured climber, who was sitting at the base of the Jackson's Thumb rappel with one obviously angulated and fractured ankle and the other severely sprained. They provided first aid and splinted both ankles. EMS personnel, rangers, and volunteer climbers then carried her a considerable distance down the descent gully and over the access trail to a point where she was transported from the scene by Life Flight helicopter.

ANALYSIS

Many climbs at City of Rocks and Castle Rocks require one or more rappels for descents. Knowledge of the number and location of rappel stations is critical. While many climbs at both parks can be done with a 60-meter rope, this is not always the case; plus, some descents may require a diagonal rappel or tension traverse to link stations.

When relocating during a rappel–either because an anchor was missed (as in this incident) or because the descent requires moving between stations–it is often reasonable to protect yourself by maintaining the rappel as you move across low-angle terrain. A third-hand backup should be used, and care must be taken to address any slack that accumulates by pulling it through the device as you move. This should only be done on very easy ground, because it is difficult to manage the ropes and climb at the same time. (*Sources: Stephen King, ranger at City of Rocks National Reserve, and the Editors.*)

KENTUCKY

CLEANING ERROR | Belayer Dragged by Climber
Red River Gorge, Muir Valley

My partner (49) and I (33) are very experienced climbers. I've climbed at the Red several times, and though it was my partner's first time here, he has climbed and belayed plenty of steep routes. My background is multi-pitch trad, and his is all sport. We are about the same weight.

On September 8, my partner led The Fury (5.11c sport) at Bibliothek in the Muir. I was tired and didn't feel like climbing the route, so we decided he would clean it while lowering off. He was clipped into the belayer's side of the rope with a quickdraw (a.k.a. tramming), as is standard practice when cleaning overhanging routes. At the last draw he said, "You're going to swing," so I weighted the rope as much as I could before he cleaned the lowest draw.

I was prepared to swing a few feet, but when he removed the last draw from the route, he was still clipped into my side of the rope. This caused both of us to swing about 20 feet backward. I slammed into a small boulder lying on the ground and then hit a tree. I made contact with one leg just above the ankle, and I think I hit my foot too. It all hurt right away. I was able to stand and walk slowly, so we hiked out.

I could barely walk for two weeks, and it took months before I was back to climbing. It was not fractured, but likely a severe bone bruise and tendonitis. (*Source: Amanda Friedman.*)

ANALYSIS

Cleaning the last draw while lowering from an overhanging route is always potentially hazardous, as the climber generally will swing out from the wall. To avoid pulling the belayer into a swing as well, the cleaning climber should completely disconnect from the belayer's side of the rope before letting go from the wall. The belayer can relocate to a good position to brace for the swing when the climber unclips the lowest bolt.

Another option is to leave the first draw on the route while cleaning and then remove it from the ground with a stick clip. (There are video tutorials online for most types of stick clips.) Muir Valley even has a few stick clips available for climbers to borrow, located underneath the awning by the parking lot. (*Source: The Editors.*)

EDITOR'S NOTE: *For detailed information on how to clean overhanging routes while lowering, see Know the Ropes on page 10.*

The climber has clipped in direct to her lowest draw on The Fury and has unclipped the belayer's side of the rope. Once the belayer takes up slack, the climber can clean the draw without causing the belayer to swing. *Johnny Nowell*

VARIOUS LEADER FALLS WITH INJURIES
Red River Gorge

On October 13, a climber swung into the wall after taking a lead fall on Air-Ride Equipped (5.11a sport) at Solarium in Muir Valley, resulting in a broken and dislocated ankle.

On October 16, an experienced female climber fell off Push Present (5.11d sport) at the Infirmary in Miller Fork. She had veered left of the bolt line, because she thought she was in the fall zone of a climber on the crux of the adjacent route (the routes share a start). Instead of climbing back down and right to get in sequence on the route, she took an unannounced fall. She swung into the wall hard, resulting in a pilon fracture.

On November 28, a female climber with over five years of experience took a controlled lead fall on The King Lives On (5.10b sport) at the Gallery in the PMRP. She hit the wall with her leg extended, resulting in a pilon fracture.

On November 30, a female climber was climbing Omaha Beach (5.14a sport) at the Motherlode. Her foot slipped, causing her leg to go behind the rope. While correcting her leg position during the fall, she inverted. Although the route is overhanging, she impacted the wall, injuring her sacrum. (*Sources: Erik Kloeker, Wolfe County Search and Rescue, eyewitness, Mountain Project, and anonymous climber.*)

ANALYSIS
Some of these injuries may have resulted from poor or unlucky positioning by the climber or inadequate awareness while falling or preparation to absorb the impact. Others might have been avoided with a softer catch by the belayer.

The arrest of a leader fall is a dynamic situation. Before the leader leaves the ground, the climber and belayer need to consider and discuss their weight difference, the properties of the rope (stretch/elongation), and any potential hazards of a fall on that route. During the climb, a skilled belayer will adjust the amount of slack in the system, their position, and their planned reaction to a fall to give an appropriate catch. (*See "Dynamic Belaying" on next page.*) The falling climber should be actively spotting their landing and preparing to absorb the impact of the fall with their legs.

Falling is part of climbing, and good partners practice their falling and belaying, just like other climbing skills. Consider practice falls at the gym or at a safe location outside, starting with falls at or below a bolt and gradually taking longer falls (when high enough on a route to be safe). This is a great time for partners to discuss their personal preferences, gauge the effects of weight differences, learn the characteristics of the climbing rope, learn how belay adjustments affect the catch, and discuss situations where a softer or tighter belay would be more appropriate. (*Source: The Editors.*)

GROUND FALL | Belay Error
Red River Gorge, Muir Valley

Around noon on October 3, a climber took a lead fall near the top of Trundling Kentucky (5.7 sport) at the Bruise Brothers Wall. The belayer failed to arrest the leader's fall, resulting in a 35- to 40-foot ground fall onto rocky terrain at the base of the climb. Eyewitnesses reported the climber impacted at free-fall speed and that the rope whipped through the quickdraws but did not seem to slow the fall.

Climbers who responded, along with Erik Kloeker of Wolfe County Search and

DYNAMIC BELAYING
THE ART OF THE SOFT CATCH

By Lindsay Auble

Lead climbing is a two-person sport. Arguably, the climber has the easy job–they climb and try not to let go. The belayer has the hard job of managing the rope and continuously planning for a fall. They are constantly evaluating the variables, adjusting the slack in the rope to make sure there is enough rope for the leader to do the moves and make efficient clips, while planning for either a short catch to keep the climber from hitting a ledge or a long catch to clear a roof or avoid a hard swing into the wall.

As the belayer, it's our job to understand the system and how our reactions change the dynamics of the fall. The belayer can influence two aspects of a fall: the length (how far the climber falls) and the hardness/softness (the rate at which the climber slows). This is done with a combination of adjusting slack and moving into (or away from) the catch. For the purposes of this discussion, we're focusing on sport climbs, but the same principles generally apply on well-protected traditional rock climbs.

When the leader is low to the ground or is at risk of hitting a ledge, tree, or other obstacle, the belayer must limit slack and be prepared to give a short, immediate catch. In extreme cases, the belayer may even pull rope out of the system or move quickly away from the rock as the climber is falling to reduce the length of a fall. (*For an example of how a quick-thinking belayer likely saved a leader from serious injury in this way in 2020, see page 71.*) Note that a short catch is not necessarily a hard catch; in some cases, it is possible and appropriate to soften a short catch.

When the climber is well above the ground and no obvious obstacles threaten, a softer and longer catch is appropriate. A soft, longer catch can reduce the whip back into the wall and give the falling leader time to spot their landing and prepare to absorb any impact with their legs. Seasoned climbers are often able to correct poor body positioning during a fall, when given enough time to react.

Overhanging climbs may create an illusion of "nothing to hit," but in reality, the steeper the climb, the more the falling climber will pendulum back toward the wall, given a tight belay. Even falls on vertical and lower-angle climbs often benefit from a softer catch, as climbers may fall or push away from the wall, creating a small pendulum that will whip them into the wall if the belay is tight.

FRANÇOIS LEBEAU

The closer the climber is to their last bolt, the more important it is to soften and lengthen a catch (when it is safe to do so). With a tight, short catch, the climber will come into the wall quickly, giving them little time to react.

Though every fall is different, in general, softening the catch provides more benefits than adding slack. To achieve a softer catch, the belayer moves *toward* the climber as the rope tightens during the fall, lengthening but slowing the arrest. The belayer anticipating a fall can squat and then stand up and/or move toward the cliff as the rope becomes tight. Sometimes it is enough for the belayer to simply relax and allow themselves to be pulled into the fall. The belayer should be positioned underneath the first bolt so they don't swing if they're pulled into the air.

Some belayers jump up while catching a fall, but the repercussions of mistiming the jump outweigh the benefits—jumping too early can give an even harder catch to the falling leader. In most cases, actively standing up from a squatted position when the rope tightens provides plenty of movement to soften a catch.

Slack is also an important consideration for the belayer; more slack means a longer catch, but it does not necessarily mean a softer catch. The amount of slack in the system affects how far the climber will free-fall before the belayer counters with their weight. More slack reduces the angle of rotation (between the falling climber and their last protection), but also means they will be falling faster (with more force) when the fall is arrested. When the climber is high enough to be out of ground fall potential, a good rule of thumb is to maintain a shallow dip in the belay rope between the belayer and the first bolt. Usually, the rope should not droop below the knees.

Many other variables affect the dynamics of a fall, and before each climb the leader and belayer should briefly discuss any special circumstances. For example, should the belayer pay out a bit more slack as the leader clears a roof? Should they take in slack for a crux above a ledge? Other things to discuss and consider:

- **Weight difference between belayer and climber.** If the belayer is lighter than the climber, they may decrease how much they move into a catch and leave less slack out. The heavier the belayer (compared to the climber), the more important it is for them to actively soften the arrest and prevent an abrupt swing into the rock.
- **Rope characteristics.** Climbing ropes vary considerably, and a rope rated higher for "dynamic elongation" will give a softer catch but also stretch more, increasing the length of the fall.
- **Belay device.** Assisted-braking devices, like the Grigri, will arrest a fall faster and with less slippage than a tube-style device, like an ATC. The belayer using an assisted-braking device needs to be more conscious of softening the catch.
- **Friction in the system.** A rope zigzagging through draws or over rock features can emphasize a pendulum effect in a fall. Longer draws help reduce friction when there are abrupt angle changes on a climb, such as below a roof.

Especially if you're climbing with someone new, talk about your preferences for the belay as well as any issues raised by specific climbs. With practice and care, partners can quickly learn to avoid many dangerous or uncomfortable falls.

Lindsay Auble lives and climbs at the Red River Gorge, Kentucky, where dynamic belaying is an essential skill.

Rescue, determined there was a possibility of spinal injury and executed a carryout to an awaiting ambulance. Hospital scans revealed the climber had a fractured vertebra and sacrum; she was expected to make a full recovery.

The climber was not wearing a helmet, and the belayer was not wearing gloves. The belayer had been climbing for four years and was using a Mammut Smart device, which has some assisted-braking capability. The rope was a newer 9.8mm Edelweiss.

ANALYSIS
All equipment was inspected and found to be in good working order. It's suspected the belayer did not have their hands in the correct braking position during the fall, and the initial load was not adequate to engage the assisted-braking function of the device. The belayer also may have inadvertently held the device in its open position, and the slickness of a newer rope could have been a factor. Despite not wearing gloves, the belayer showed no signs of burns on the hands. Regardless of which assisted-braking belay device you use, the brake hand must retain control of the rope throughout the process of feeding out or taking in rope or catching a fall. (*Sources: Erik Kloeker, Wolfe County Search and Rescue, and the Editors.*)

MONTANA

LEADER FALL | Loose Rock, Inadequate Protection
Gallatin Canyon, The Watchtower

On August 23, Eric (64) and his climbing partner Ed (57) were planning to link the standard route up the Watchtower (5.8) with Silver Foxes (5.8) on the Watchtower's upper tier, and then finish on Spare Rib (5.8), all traditional lines on the east side of Gallatin Canyon. Both are experienced climbers. Ed led the pitches on the Watchtower and the first two pitches of Silver Foxes. The two then decided to do the alternative third pitch of Silver Foxes (5.6) instead of the standard final pitch of 5.10a/b. This pitch starts on a large ledge where a belay anchor is not needed. The variation appeared as though it was not climbed frequently.

At about 1:30 p.m., Eric started to lead. About eight feet above the belay, he came to a block that, after testing, seemed solid. Using the block as a hold, he went for the next hold with his other hand and the block pulled loose. Eric pushed the block away from Ed as he fell and, having placed no pro, dropped to the belay ledge. Landing on a sharp rock, he suffered a deep ten-inch laceration on his right calf and fractured his fibula. He tried standing up, but realized the injuries were too severe to get back down without additional help.

Ed, who is a paramedic, bandaged Erik's leg with climbing tape and webbing and moved him into the shade, anchoring him to a large tree. At 2 p.m., Ed gave Eric some food and water and left to call for help. By 2:35 p.m., Ed was at the Lava Lake emergency call-box on Highway 191 and placed a 911 call. A party of two overheard Ed phoning for help and offered to climb up to Eric while Ed waited at the parking lot. Ed gave the couple a large roll of gauze that he obtained from his car, and they climbed the first two pitches of Silver Foxes to access Eric, then used the gauze to help control the bleeding from the laceration. Eric was spotted by a Gallatin County Search and Rescue helicopter at approximately 4 p.m. and was short-hauled from the site in a litter.

ANALYSIS

The two climbers noticed that the variation seemed infrequently climbed, which could have alerted them to the possibility of loose rock and the need for greater care with the holds. In loose terrain, placing more protection should be considered, especially close to the ground or a ledge. In places where there is no cell phone coverage, a satellite communicator can dramatically speed response time if emergency assistance is needed. (*Sources: The climbers, Gallatin County SAR, and the Editors.*)

LOWERING ERROR | Rope Too Short, Complacency
Paradise Valley, Allenspur Main Crag

On March 20, a pair of climbers (Climber 1, male, 28, and Climber 2, female, 27, both intermediate-level climbers) headed to the Main Crag at Allenspur and packed their "all around" 50-meter rope, since that length is adequate for most (but not all) of the routes at the crag. They chose Climbing Club (5.8), a 90-foot sport route, for a warm-up.

Climber 1 tied in, climbed to the top without issues, and signaled Climber 2 to lower him. As Climber 1 was nearing the base of the climb, the rope end slipped through the belayer's Grigri. Climber 1 estimates he fell about 18 feet to the ground (although he has no recollection of the actual fall). The rope end had not been tied to the rope bag, nor was a stopper knot tied in the end.

A call to 911 brought emergency services to the crag, and Climber 1 was packaged into a Stokes litter and lowered a short distance down the hill to a waiting ambulance. He sustained a concussion, two fractured lumbar transverse processes (L4 and L5), a minor fracture of the left scapula, laceration of the right elbow, and pulled muscles in his right shoulder.

ANALYSIS

This accident occurred through a series of preventable errors and complacency while doing a relatively easy warm-up. Climber 1 stated: "The 50-meter rope had never been an issue before at this crag and was typically tied off to the bag when crag climbing [thereby closing the system]. Climber 1 set off under these assumptions. Recent gym use had led the pair to flipping the rope often [to allow each end to rest between falls], and they had left the rope untied during this trip to the crag." In addition, the belayer was positioned below a neighboring route, adding about 10 feet to the effective length of the climb. (*Source: Climber 1.*)

ROCKFALL, ANCHOR FAILURE
Beartooth Mountains, Granite Peak

On July 2, Emma Ely (25), Randy Smersh (36), and I (Zach Eiten, 28), all experienced mountaineers, set out to climb the Notch Couloir route on the north face of Granite Peak (12,799 feet), Montana's high point. The Notch Couloir is described as "steep snow followed by a 5.4 ridge to the summit." We approached via Huckleberry Creek, bivouacked between Avalanche and Cold lakes, and on July 3 we were underway around 4 a.m. The boulder fields surrounding Avalanche Lake slowed us significantly, and when we reached the cirque below Granite Peak, Randy decided to split off and climb the standard (east ridge) route via the Tempest-Granite saddle. We maintained contact throughout the day via walkie-talkies. Emma and I started up our

The north face of Granite Peak showing the Notch Couloir and the accident site on the north ridge. The east ridge is in the left foreground. *Gallatin County Search and Rescue*

route and simul-climbed most of the couloir with only a couple of belays.

At the saddle atop the couloir it began to snow, and we paused in case it became necessary to bail. Conditions in the Notch Couloir had been deteriorating as the daytime temperature increased (the forecast called for temperatures in the 30s to low 40s Fahrenheit), and we had seen some very small sloughs and minor rockfall, so we felt inclined to wait for the storm to pass rather than bail down the couloir.

As the squall subsided, we assessed the north ridge, which was more iced up and snow-packed than hoped, and opted for a line just to the east of the saddle in mixed condition. I started up a gully that felt like M3, with loose rock; I was able to place only a single nut and a number 1 cam. At the top of the pitch, I slung a refrigerator-size block and placed a 0.75 cam in the crack formed by the intersection of the block and the main face. I knew this belay was insecure, so I didn't weight the anchor; I had only a six- to eight-inch-wide ledge to stand on. It was around 1 p.m.

As I began pulling up the ropes to belay Emma, a microwave-size rock fell spontaneously from the gully above me. This large block and ensuing cascade of rocks collided with my anchor block and launched it off the edge. Instantly I was falling. Thankfully, the pitch below formed a series of steps, with vertical sections separated by ledges; I was able to arrest my fall on one of these ledges. Had I not done so, I would have fallen another 20 feet or more before being arrested by the cam I placed on the ascent.

One of the blocks had crushed my left foot during the barrage. I managed to place a bomber nut and sling a good horn that allowed Emma to lower me to her anchor. After confirming my toes were likely broken, I established radio contact with Randy, who was descending to the basin after retreating from his route, and asked him to try to contact search and rescue.

Emma and I began rappelling the Notch Couloir. It took six 70-meter rappels to reach the snow apron at the base. My foot was quite numb at this point, which allowed me to cautiously glissade and heel-step down the snowfield. We reached snowline around sunset, and at 3 a.m. we arrived back at our base camp.

Meanwhile, Randy had encountered a party at Huckleberry Lake who used their Garmin inReach to initiate a rescue. Around 7 a.m., Two Bear Air, a philanthropic rescue crew, arrived in a helicopter but were unable to land due to strong winds. Gallatin County SAR, on standby, responded shortly after and was able to land its helicopter near our camp. I was flown to Absarokee, Montana, where an ambulance took me to a clinic for X-rays. I had multiple broken bones in four of the five toes on my left foot.

ANALYSIS

The natural rockfall was very unfortunate. I cannot say what would have happened had I remained anchored when the rocks fell onto my position, but at the end of the day I made the mistake of settling for a subpar anchor. The slung block and the cam placed between it and the wall both failed when the block dislodged, so the anchor was not actually redundant. I could have pounded my ice tools in cracks or turf and/or tried to excavate a secondary feature to find protection that would have affixed me to the mountain as well as to the boulder.

Another factor was the lack of solid freeze on mixed terrain. The fact that we'd been slowed throughout the day (the boulder field, waiting out the brief snowstorm) meant the temperature was higher than it would have been if I'd reached this stance earlier in the day. Every now and again while mixed climbing you reach an anchor position with less than ideal gear, and massive blocks or relatively sketchy horns become your friends. However, this is generally when everything is frozen over in late fall or winter, and in the afternoon in early July, Granite Peak was far from solidly frozen. (*Source: Zach Eiten.*)

FALL ON SNOW AND ANCHOR FAILURE
Beartooth Mountains, Granite Peak

Two falls occurred on September 5 on the east ridge, the standard route up Granite Peak, one of them resulting in a fatality.

At about 2 p.m., Jay (22) slipped while crossing a narrow col known as the Snowbridge and slid 250 feet down a snow gully and into steep scree. He suffered several broken ribs, a broken collarbone, a small closed pneumothorax, and numerous lacerations and bruises.

Jay's partner, Jared (19), descended to Froze to Death Plateau to try to get cell phone service, and at the plateau encountered another party, who used their inReach to call for help. Meanwhile, Heather (23) and Miles (30), both EMTs and Big Sky ski patrollers, were descending from higher on the mountain when the incident occurred. They downclimbed to Jay and provided emergency care. At around 8 p.m., a Montana National Guard helicopter tried to insert a rescuer to the scene, but due to the wind, elevation, and coming nightfall, the flight was suspended. Jay, Miles, and Heather prepared to bivouac for the night.

At around 5 p.m. that same day, four climbers (three males in their 40s and one male in his 60s) were descending the east ridge after reaching the summit around 3:30 p.m. This group was experienced and equipped with a rope, a rock rack, food, water, cell phones, and warm clothes. The descent features two optional rappels of about 80 feet each. At their second rappel, the party chose to use an existing anchor with webbing around a boulder. Climber 1 was about 30 feet into the rappel when the entire boulder dislodged and fell down the face; he fell a short distance to a small ledge, where he was able to stop his fall, but suffered injuries to both ankles. Climber 2, who was standing below the boulder, waiting to rappel, was knocked off balance when the boulder came loose, and he fell approximately 1,000 feet.

Granite Peak from the south. (A) Location of climber after fall from the Snowbridge, the saddle in the east ridge directly above. (B) Site of rappel anchor failure. (C) Position of fallen climber. *Gallatin County Search and Rescue*

Climber 3 and Climber 4 were able to downclimb to Climber 1 and recover the rope, which they used to move him to a more secure location. Climber 3 then used the rope to descend to Climber 2 and confirm he had died in the fall. The climbers were able to reach 911 by phone at 5:30 p.m. Climbers 1 and 4 bivouacked at their location, and Climber 3 bivouacked at the lower location with his deceased partner.

On September 6 at 7:10 a.m. the Gallatin County Search and Rescue helicopter inserted rescuers at both the upper and lower accident sites. By around 8:30 a.m., Climbers 1 through 4, Jay, Heather, and Miles all had been extricated to a staging area. By around 10 a.m., all parties involved were off the mountain.

ANALYSIS

Although the east ridge route (a.k.a. east ridge to south face) is rated as 4th class, trip reports and guidebooks warn that route-finding can be difficult on the upper mountain, and the terrain is quite exposed in places—it is definitely not a "walkup." Depending on the comfort level and experience of climbing parties, a rope and a light rock rack and slings can be useful to protect exposed sections and reinforce rappel anchors. In late season, the Snowbridge is often melted out, but earlier in the year, an ice axe and crampons will make this passage more secure. Jay and Jared were inexperienced for a route of this difficulty and carried no technical equipment.

Fixed rappel anchors should always be carefully assessed and tested before trusting one's life to them. In this case, a firm test-push might have revealed the instability of the boulder and prevented the tragic incident. Note that the first person to reach a rappel anchor should inspect and test the anchor setup *before* clipping to the anchor; if necessary, this test should be performed while protected by a temporary anchor or while still clipped to the ropes from the previous rappel. See "Know the Ropes: Rappelling" (2012) for tips on setting up and assessing rappel anchors, and "Know the Ropes: Safer 4th Class" (2018) for ideas on moving safely and efficiently through such terrain; both articles are available at *publications.americanalpineclub. org*. (*Sources: Gallatin County Search and Rescue and the Editors.*)

NEVADA

GROUND FALL | Downclimbing 4th-Class Terrain
Red Rock Canyon National Conservation Area, Oak Creek Canyon

On October 31 at approximately 7 a.m., my climbing partner and I set out to climb Solar Slab in Oak Creek Canyon. At about 8:30 a.m. we arrived at the base of a large gully in the Lower Solar Slab area. [*Editor's Note: Solar Slab, a classic multi-pitch 5.6, is generally accessed by climbing the Solar Slab Gully, which has about 500 feet of low 5th-class terrain. The gully leads to a large ledge, which serves as the start for numerous climbs, including the actual route Solar Slab.*]

By 10 a.m. I had led three rope lengths and my partner had led half a rope length, totaling approximately 650 feet. At this point, we realized the climb we had done was not aligning with the route description for the Solar Slab Gully. We decided we must have gone off route at some point and chose to retreat back down the gully we had climbed.

We had executed two rappels when we encountered 25 to 30 feet of 4th-class terrain. To save time, we opted to downclimb this section. At about 11 a.m., while at the top of the downclimb, I slipped and fell the entire length of the 4th-class section, landing on a large flat area below. According to my climbing partner, I hit a bush and then landed on my face/head. I was wearing a helmet, which exploded upon impact. I was briefly unconscious, and when I came to, I was barely able to communicate. My condition worsened with time.

My climbing partner immediately contacted search and rescue, and they arrived about three hours after the fall. I got to the hospital at 3:20 p.m. I had sustained a major brain hemorrhage, multiple skull fractures, a fractured distal radius in my right wrist, and a dislocated pinkie. Six months later, I had fully recovered, outside of some loss of right wrist mobility.

ANALYSIS
Several factors contributed to the accident. First and foremost, we had gotten off route from the start. We arrived in Las Vegas late the prior evening and hadn't closely studied the approach to Solar Slab Gully, the relative location of the gully to Solar Slab itself, nor the features on each of the pitches on Solar Slab Gully. Had we done this preparation, we would have either gotten on the correct climb or quickly determined we were on the wrong climb and retreated sooner.

On the descent, we should have continued rappelling down the gully instead of opting to downclimb the 4th-class section. Part of what pushed us to downclimb was that we wanted to descend the gully quickly, so we would have time to find our way to the Solar Slab climb.

Another factor that contributed to the accident was confirmation bias. I was used to downclimbing a 30-foot section of 4th-class terrain at my home crag at Seneca Rocks, West Virginia. This gave me false confidence in high-consequence terrain. (*Source: Anonymous report from the climber.*)

NEW HAMPSHIRE

ROCKFALL | Severed Rope
White Mountains, Cannon Cliff

On September 20, Ben Kessel (34) and Emma Leigh Donahue (30s) were climbing Moby Grape (8 pitches, 5.8 PG-13) on Cannon Cliff. Both were active within the MIT Outing Club and experienced rock climbers. Conditions were windy but pleasant, and there had been no rain for days. As is common on summer and early fall weekends, multiple parties were climbing the route; Ben and Emma were the first, and highest, party. Kevin Soleil and Bill Moriarty were climbing as a separate party just below and left of Ben and Emma throughout the day and witnessed this accident.

Ben had climbed the route before and was informally mentoring Emma, who was new to Cannon. They swapped leads and most of the climb went uneventfully, although they did have some difficulty managing rope drag at places and Emma took one short fall. Around 3:30 p.m., Emma reached the top of pitch seven after taking a slightly different route than the most commonly climbed line. (The upper pitches of many climbs at Cannon present route-finding challenges as the angle gradually lessens.) At about 3:45 p.m., as she was belaying Ben up to her stance, a block estimated to be the size of a refrigerator became dislodged about 50 feet below the belay and fell directly toward Ben as he approached from below. The rock slid over their single rope, severing it and knocking Ben off the route into a long free fall.

At the time of the incident, Kevin had just reached the top of Kurt's Corner, an alternate finish about 75 feet to the left. Kevin heard Ben shout "Rock!" and he got a brief glancing view of the rock falling. Emma, Bill, and another climbing party below who overheard the incident promptly called 911. New Hampshire Fish and Game and Pemigewasset Valley SAR personnel were subsequently notified and began their response toward both the base of the cliff and the summit area.

After the rockfall stopped, Kevin quickly belayed Bill to his location and they traversed to Emma's belay stance to provide assistance. Together, the three carefully rappelled down to search for and try to help Ben. They took care to avoid the immediate rockfall site to prevent dislodging any additional material. At 5:30 p.m., Emma located Ben on a ledge about 150 feet below the rockfall site among some small, dense spruce trees. Kevin soon also reached this site. Ben had not survived the fall.

Kevin, Emma, and Bill ascended their ropes, and responders reached the scene at 6:15 p.m., with only about 30 minutes of daylight remaining. Given the impending darkness, they focused on assisting the uninjured climbers to the top of the cliff before night fell and temperatures dropped. Early the next morning, responders from New Hampshire Fish and Game, Mountain Rescue Service, and Pemi Valley SAR completed the recovery.

ANALYSIS

Cannon is a large alpine cliff subject to both climber-triggered and spontaneous rockfall. The current Cannon guidebook (Sykes, 2017) describes the recent history of specific rockfalls and climber accidents in detail (pp. 180–186). In 1968, a climber died while placing a piton behind a block, causing it to fall onto him. In 1988, two climbers were killed when the rock supporting their belay anchors failed, causing them to fall to the ground. In 2006, a climber was severely injured when a block he was standing on released and caused a long fall (see ANAC 2007). While spontaneous natural rockfall is common, the only known incident of natural rockfall resulting in a climber injury was in the early 1990s, when massive rockfall starting high on the cliff shattered and reached climbers on the talus slopes far below.

Since neither Emma nor Kevin had a clear view of the block as it started falling, the immediate cause cannot be determined. However, climber-triggered rockfall cannot be ruled out. Cultivating an awareness of potential loose blocks and conditions that increase rockfall hazard is a must for those choosing to climb on Cannon and similar alpine crags. Early season is particularly hazardous, due to springtime wetness and freeze-thaw cycling, as is climbing immediately after heavy rain. Getting off route can increase the exposure to loose rock. Hollow sounding rocks, newly exposed sharp, clean edges, or gaps should raise suspicion. In general, avoid pulling on, standing on, placing protection around, or allowing ropes to drag against any suspicious rocks.

The hazard of rockfall severing the climbing rope could be somewhat mediated by using double-rope technique (two half ropes); skillful use of half ropes may also give the leader more options to bypass an area of suspicious rock.

This incident is a sobering reminder of the rockfall hazard on even the most popular Cannon routes. It's also important to remember that climbing below other parties on multi-pitch routes exposes climbers to a high risk of human-triggered rockfall and other falling objects. (*Sources: Kevin Soleil, Bill Moriarty, New Hampshire Fish and Game Department, and the Editors.*)

GROUND FALL | Improvised Harness Failure
Rumney, Parking Lot Wall

On September 25, at about 4 p.m., a climber (age 68) was attempting to climb Dead Sea Equestrian (5.7 sport) at the Parking Lot Wall of Rumney. Near the top, approximately 50 feet above the base, he called for his belayer to "take" his weight onto the rope. As he weighted the belay system, his harness separated from the rope and he fell to the ground. Many nearby climbers immediately responded to the fallen climber and notified emergency medical personnel, who responded quickly. Despite their efforts, the climber was pronounced dead at the scene.

ANALYSIS
According to his belayer, the climber had forgotten to put his climbing harness in his car when he drove from his home, two hours away. He decided to improvise one out of kayak straps additionally secured with a leather belt. The DIY harness failed under body weight and separated from the rope where the leather belt broke at the buckle holes.

Although it is possible to improvise a "diaper sling" harness if climbers have appropriate webbing and other materials, this alternative will never be as secure nor as comfortable as a UIAA-certified climbing harness in good condition. A verbal or written checklist to remember critical items before leaving home could have prevented this incident. Sadly, the climber declined to borrow a harness that was offered by another climber in the parking lot. Additionally, there is a sporting equipment shop within 10 miles of this crag where a replacement harness could have been purchased. (*Source: Lt. James Kneeland, New Hampshire Fish and Game.*)

FALL ON SNOW | Inadequate Equipment
Mt. Washington, Tuckerman Ravine

A ski mountaineer fell several hundred feet down Chute in Tuckerman Ravine while attempting to approach a ski descent using inadequate crampons and no ice axe. *Jamie Walter*

Around noon on March 9, the AMC Hermit Lake caretaker reported seeing a person "tomahawking"–i.e., falling end over end–the length of the gully called Chute in Tuckerman Ravine. The caretaker and a snow ranger responded and were pleased to find the patient had no apparent injuries. The person walked to Hermit Lake and was assisted down to the road by snow machine.

It was reported that at the time of the fall the man was climbing near the top of Chute wearing leather boots with micro-spikes and no ice tool. He carried ski boots and skis on his backpack. The snow was still firm, barely softened by the sun.

ANALYSIS
Safe climbing of steep snow–especially hard snow–requires stiff boots and the skilled use of crampons and an ice axe (or two) to prevent a fall. When climbing without the protection of a rope and belay, preventing a fall is a climber or skier's primary means of safety, since arresting a fall a steep, hard snow is difficult with an ice axe and impossible without. (*Source: Mount Washington Avalanche Center.*)

NEW MEXICO

LOOSE ROCK
Cactus Chimney Boulders

On February 21, Callaway Lewis (female, age 8), her older brother, and her father, Anthony, were climbing around the Cactus Chimney Boulders, one of several small bouldering areas just east of the city limits, when the rock Callaway was climbing slid, pinning her between two boulders. Anthony was able to free Callaway and extract her from the foothills to the nearby road. She sustained a broken pelvis in multiple locations, several spinal fractures, spleen lacerations, a broken femur, shattered tibia and fibula, and a shattered right foot, resulting in amputation.

ANALYSIS

Weathering of granite in the Sandia Mountains foothills accelerates during the winter and early spring due to continual freeze-thaw cycles on the west side of the Sandias, and rockfall and rock movement are most common in these months. As this tragic accident shows, past use of a hold or boulder does not guarantee its stability in the future. (*Sources: News reports and the Editors.*)

NEW YORK

SHAWANGUNKS ANNUAL SUMMARY
Monhonk Preserve

In 2020 the Mohonk Preserve experienced a statistically anomalous year due to the COVID-19 pandemic. For two months, the land was closed to visitors and no access passes were sold. When the preserve was open, there was a significant increase in non-climbing day passes. Meanwhile, the access passes that allow climbing saw a marked decrease, especially from the shutdown until October (when the numbers returned to pre-pandemic levels.) These changes are reflected in the report below.

Mohonk Preserve rangers responded to 11 climbing-related accidents in 2020. (By contrast, there were 22 reported accidents in 2019 and 23 in 2018.) There was one fatality. The other accidents resulted in two head injuries, five lower-leg injuries, one pelvic fracture, and assorted minor lacerations. One rappelling climber was bitten by a copperhead and was evacuated after safely getting themselves to the carriage road. Five climbing incidents required technical rescue, and two of those were high-angle. Rangers were also deployed seven other times for technical rescue in non-climbing accidents from difficult terrain.

The fatality occurred on the route Triple Bulges, a 5.6 route in the Trapps. The leader was approximately 90 feet above the Guide's Wall Ledge, and had placed several pieces of protection along their route. Here, at one of the crux sections over a small roof, the leader placed at least one more camming device (it was recovered after the incident and did not appear to have been clipped to the rope.) The leader fell from this point, and several camming devices pulled out of the rock, failing to arrest the fall before the leader struck a ledge 20 feet above their belayer. Nearby climbers and rangers responded quickly, but the resulting technical work was a recovery.

In two other accidents, lead climbers had protection pieces fail in falls, but were protected from more serious injury by lower elements of the system. One leader placed a camming unit and then fell before clipping it. The quick actions of their belayer and the lower pieces minimized the injuries sustained (*see report below*).

One leader fell a short distance at the start of the first pitch of Annie Oh! (5.8+) in the Trapps and suffered a tibia/fibula fracture. Despite the climber being close to the ground, responding rangers devised a high-angle lower to get the seriously injured person down from a ledge only accessible by 4th-class movement.

A rappeler attempting to access the anchor bolts at the top of Bunny (5.4) used an unknown method to attach their rope to a small pitch pine tree on top of the cliff. (The anchor bolts are 20 feet below the walkable clifftop.) When the rappeler weighted the system, the rope unraveled from the tree and they fell 15 feet to a sloping ledge above the bolts (and far off the ground.) Rangers completed a high-angle rescue to reach the climber and lower them to the carriage road.

One climber was involved in a non-climbing accident that resulted in severe head and back injuries when the hammock they were attempting to enter broke apart. The hammock had been suspended from trees over a steep talus field. Mohonk Preserve rules do not allow hammocks to be attached to trees.

ANALYSIS
Accidents on the Mohonk Preserve dropped 50 percent from the previous climbing season. There are several theoretical explanations for this. Perhaps there were fewer climbers overall (as noted in the statistics that are mentioned above). Perhaps the climbers who decided to come to the Preserve were more conservative in their objectives and risk management or they represented a more experienced segment of the climbing population at large.

One notable observation is that a majority of the incidents in 2020 were the result of climber error. Absent are reports of rockfall-related accidents, and there was only one event that involved environmental dangers (a snakebite). Also absent from years past are stranded climbers who found themselves unprepared or off route.

This overview of the incidents that occurred in the Mohonk Preserve serves as a reminder to stay up to date on the variety of skills necessary to be safe, even in an area with very convenient access. (*Source: Mohonk Preserve Rangers, Andrew Bajardi, Chief Ranger.*)

FALL ON ROCK | Inadequate Protection
Shawangunks, The Trapps

On August 30, I (male, 59) started up Pas de Deux (5.8 PG-13). I placed two or three good cams in the first 20 feet of the climb. Above that, I saw a couple of places I could have placed cams, not far above my highest piece, but decided to move higher before placing another one. Looking up, I could see horizontal corrugations, but upon reaching them they turned out not to be deep enough to accept cams. At roughly 35 feet, I first tried to place a blue Metolius TCU, but the placement was poor. I then tried to place a purple TCU in the same crack, a little to the left. I gave it a tug and it popped out, which caused me to lose my balance and fall. I flipped upside down and fell about 25 feet. When the rope came taut, the back of my helmet hit the wall as I neared the ground.

I'd abraded my right hand and finger, bruised my pelvis, and sustained a deep cut on my elbow. I remained conscious and alert and was greatly relieved to have sustained only minor injuries. The helmet seemed to have absorbed the impact to my head. A number of Mohonk Preserve rangers were climbing nearby and immediately attended to me. After the fall I was woozy, with low blood pressure and a slow pulse. I was carried to the carriage road in a litter and taken to the hospital to be checked out.

ANALYSIS

I was comfortable standing on good footholds for about five minutes while attempting to place various small cams and finally the purple one that pulled out. When I tested it, I let my guard down a bit in a dangerous situation, when I should have been as careful and alert as if I were free soloing, given the distance above my last good pro.

I owe huge thanks to my belayer Nathan (whom I'd just met through Mountain Project) for running backward from his stance as I fell, removing just enough slack from the system to prevent a much more serious injury. (*Source: Christopher Maher.*)

NORTH CAROLINA

STRANDED | Climbing Alone, Exhaustion
Stone Mountain State Park

During the late afternoon on October 1, a solo climber notified 911 and reported he was uninjured but physically exhausted and unable to finish his climb. He said he was high on the second pitch of the Great Arch (3 pitches, 5.5). Wilkes County dispatch was notified, and a high-angle team was sent to help evacuate him. After reaching the summit area, rescuers contacted the climber and one team member descended to meet the climber, who was then assisted to the top. (*Lynette Hicks, ranger, Stone Mountain State Park.*)

ANALYSIS

Although the falling hazards of free soloing are obvious, incidents like this, in which a climber runs out of nerve or stamina, also happen every year around North America. Such strandings frequently occur on long but technically moderate climbs, suggesting soloists underestimate their readiness for such climbs. (*Source: The Editors.*)

GROUND FALL | Protection Pulled Out
Pilot Mountain State Park

On August 1 a party of three, Michael Hall (26), M. Johnson (26), and D. Jones (28), were climbing Cowboys and Heroes (5.7), a 40-foot route in the Foreign Trade Zone area. Hall was leading the route and fell from a harder variation near the top of the climb after he weighted his highest piece and it pulled out. In the resulting ground fall, Hall suffered open fractures of the tibia and fibula on his right leg, a laceration to the left leg, and a fractured sternum.

Hall described what happened: We arrived at Pilot Mountain around 9:30 a.m. and got on a trad climb to warm up, and followed with some top-roping and projecting two 5.10s. Around 11:20 a.m., we moved to a new area and I decided to attempt to onsight Cowboys and Heroes.

I placed my first piece at around 10 feet in a horizontal crack. The next 10 feet of climbing leads to a ledge 18 to 20 feet from ground. The second placement was a blue number 1 TCU, also in a horizontal crack. I tested this piece by grabbing the sling and giving it two quick jerks. The final portion of the climb has a number of finishes. Rather than take the 5.7 finish as I had intended, I started working up a vertical crack (5.10).

At this point, with my feet approximately 25 to 30 feet from the ground, I started to get pumped. I placed a clearly under-cammed (tipped out) number 2 cam, and as the pump intensified, I began looking for a placement to back it up. While trying to grab a number 3 cam from my rack, my arms began to give out. I grabbed the draw attached to the number 2 cam to help me place the larger piece, but this resulted in the number 2 cam pulling out. As I fell, the blue TCU also pulled from the rock. I fell past the ledge, hitting my left knee on the way down, and landed on the ground with both my feet taking the full force of the fall, before falling backward and coming to a rest on my back and side.

One of my partners tried to immobilize me while the other called 911. A climbing guide and off-duty fireman were in the area and reached me within a few minutes. A ranger and Surry County EMS responded to the 911 call, and I was transported to a waiting ambulance. (*Sources: Michael Hall and Pilot Mountain State Park ranger Jesse A. Anderson.*)

The route Cowboys and Heroes is interrupted by several ledges, requiring a leader to place abundant and solid protection for a safe ascent. *Evan McKearn*

ANALYSIS

Hall noted: "I believe that not placing additional gear, climbing on rock that had moisture and was dirty, and not staying on route were the factors contributing to my fall. By downclimbing five feet or so [to regroup], I may have been able to prevent the fall. Luckily, I was wearing a helmet. A life-changing accident can happen on an easy climb as quickly as it can on a hard one."

Many climbers opt to top-rope the traditionally protected routes at Pilot Mountain because bands of poor rock exist throughout the climbing area. In addition, the routes are often quite short, making a ground fall a real possibility when cam or nut placements fail. (*Sources: Michael Hall and the Editors.*)

LOOSE ROCK | Weather, Seldom-Climbed Route
Hanging Rock State Park, Moore's Wall, Sentinel Buttress

On May 27, following a two-week period of heavy rain, a pair of very experienced climbers planned to do the popular route Break on Through (5.10a) on the Circus Wall of Sentinel Buttress. The route begins from a ledge approximately 60 feet up an adjacent wall; to reach the start, climbers ascend easy 5th-class terrain on the Egg Wall or the Sentinel Chimney. On this day, both of the usual approaches were soaking wet with runoff. However, the climbers noted a large dry streak on the Egg Wall, along or near a seldom-traveled route known as Scrambled Eggs (approximately 5.6). Above them, Break on Through was almost completely dry and judged to be climbable.

Climber 1 led the pitch to the ledge and built a solid belay anchor. Climber 2 was following the pitch, approximately 30 feet off the ground, when he reached a rounded fin of rock that he needed for a handhold to clear a small overhang. The hold appeared to be an integral part of the wall, but since it was clear that the recent rains had loosened a lot of holds, Climber 2 tested it by partially weighting the hold overhead and bouncing with his body weight. He felt some movement in the rock, tested it again, and felt no further movement—since he was on easy ground, he judged it was safe to continue. As he moved off his stance, the rock gave way and a piece approximately 14 inches square and weighing about 25 pounds hit him on the head (he was wearing a helmet), knee, and finally on the top of his right foot.

Despite his foot injury, Climber 2 was able to traverse about 50 feet to a rappel station on an adjacent route, protecting the traverse using the gear on his harness. Climber 1 followed the improvised traverse, and then both climbers rappelled and hiked out. An X-ray revealed a fracture of the first metatarsal. (*Source: Climber 2.*)

ANALYSIS

Substantial wet weather or freeze-thaw cycles may cause seemingly solid holds to work loose. These experienced climbers understood the potential impact of heavy rain on the variable quartzite at Moore's Wall; they altered their usual approach to avoid wet rock, and they tested suspect holds. After feeling the hold move when he tested it the first time, the climber might have tried to find an alternative line. Yet this might have led him onto other seldom-climbed terrain, with other loose holds.

"It's easy to forget at popular areas, where the classics have 40 years of traffic and little loose rock, that wandering even just a few feet off the beaten path can lead to a first-ascent-like experience, in terms of rock quality," Climber 2 said. "We often free solo a clean and well-traveled easy section of this wall as an approach pitch, so it's tempting to treat the whole wall as a foregone conclusion. That led to a case of experienced climbers not adjusting expectations to current conditions." (*Sources: Climber 2 and the Editors.*)

LONG FALL | Carabiner Unclipped After Stick-Clipping
Linville Gorge, Hawksbill Mountain

On June 14, I was belaying a very experienced climber who was attempting to stick-clip through the crux on a route. The climber clipped the second bolt from the ground and then began to pull up on the belay strand of the rope while I pulled in slack. I heard a metallic ping sound and watched the climber fall. I dove off a ledge to take up slack, and the climber came very close to a ground fall, but ended up with only some abrasions.

The dogbone on the quickdraw had somehow detached itself from the carabiner clipped to the second bolt. I went up and retrieved the carabiner and it looked normal, and the dogbone looked A-OK as well. My only conclusion is that while the climber was going hand over hand up the rope, he inadvertently shifted the draw into a kind of "back clip" position in which the nylon dogbone could open the gate of the carabiner and work free. (*Source: Anonymous belayer.*)

ANALYSIS

Stick-clipping is a great way to protect the opening moves of a climb or to get a top-rope up on a hard sport climb so you can work out the moves. But this also can create an illusion of safety, and it's important not to be complacent about clipping bolts or double-checking the results. When climbers opt to stick-clip the second bolt of a route, it's a good idea to clip the first as well, as backup. (*Source: The Editors.*)

GROUND FALL | Excess Slack, Fatigue, Missed Clip
Melrose Mountain Climbing Park

Melrose Mountain is a relatively new climbing area, near the South Carolina border, that hosts top-rope, trad, mixed, and sport routes (5.7–5.11). On December 19, Jesse Watson (32) and his partner EC (31) were finishing their day by climbing Feelin' Good (5.10a), a 50-foot, five-bolt sport route. Jesse was leading and had clipped the first three bolts on the route without difficulty. At the fourth bolt, he struggled to clip and kept dropping the rope. At this point, he knew he "was going to fall" and noted that he was high enough on the route that a ground fall was not expected to be an issue. He lost his grip and fell approximately 30 to 35 feet to the ground. He was not wearing a helmet.

His belayer, using a Grigri Plus, had given him slack to make the clip and was unable to pull in the slack and arrest his fall before he impacted the large boulder beneath the climb, hitting feet first. (The rope didn't catch him until he came to rest in a seated position.) A paramedic, Jesse did a quick self-assessment and found an open fracture of his left tibia/fibula and a suspected fractured right ankle.

ANALYSIS

Jesse described what he had learned from this incident: "I think what it ultimately came down to was complacency. I am very comfortable leading 5.10 sport, and my partner and I had become too comfortable with the fact that I *don't* fall. I usually climb pretty fast, so I had requested extra slack from my belayer so as to not get hung up. The additional slack for the clip, the distance my belayer was standing from the face due to the boulder below the route, and fatigue were all factors in this accident. I was not wearing a helmet and was extremely lucky to 'walk away' with the injuries I did."

When belayers position themselves anywhere but directly under the climb, it's not just the climber at risk—the belayer can be pulled into the wall by the forces of a fall, causing serious injuries. When the topography forces you to belay more than a few feet away from an ideal position, consider a ground anchor. (*Sources: Jesse Watson and the Editors.*)

ANOTHER GROUND FALL AT MELROSE: *In August, a climber experienced a ground fall on a route next to Feelin' Good. He did the first few moves of Something to BRAG About (5.11- trad) and placed a medium cam in an undercling. Deciding he couldn't make the next moves, he asked to rest on the cam, but as soon as he weighted it, the bottom of the flake snapped off and he fell to the ground. "Luckily my belayer spotted me and kept my body from landing weird," he said. "I had just a scrape on my arm." The climber said he failed to notice a small crack in the rock near his placement, and that he now plans to climb only sport routes at this crag because of the rock quality. (Source: Anonymous climber.)*

OREGON

LOST AND STRANDED | Weather, Hypothermia
Mt. Hood, South Side

A team heads out in deep snow and poor visibility during an extended operation to rescue a snowboard mountaineer who got lost and hypothermic during his descent on Mt. Hood. *Portland Mountain Rescue*

On May 22, a snowboarder (male, 31) lost his bearings in whiteout conditions while descending from a summit attempt and had to spend the night out, leading to a severe case of hypothermia.

According to a post he made at Facebook after these events, it had not been the climber's intention to summit the mountain, but it was a beautiful day and he decided he had the gear and stamina to head for the top. However, the weather changed drastically during the ascent, from partly sunny to extremely low visibility. As he headed down in a whiteout, he deviated from the normal route toward Timberline Lodge and descended the fall line farther west toward the cliffs of Mississippi Head. In waist-deep snow, he attempted to use the Find My Car app on his phone to guide him toward the parking area. However, he still had a long way to go in rugged terrain, and when his phone was nearly out of life, he used the last of his battery to call 911 at around 8:30 p.m.

While he waited for help, the man dug a snow cave behind a big rock and lined it with fir boughs from the only tree in his area. He attempted to light a fire, but was unsuccessful in the wind and driving rain. He conserved the little food he had and waited.

Around 10 p.m., seven members of Portland Mountain Rescue (PMR) assembled at the day lodge at Timberline. It was decided to send a team of six to the top of the Palmer ski lift and head out from there to rescue the man, using the GPS coordinates from his phone. Travel was slow due to the deep snow. As they neared the man's location, the team started doing whistle blasts. On the second whistle, they got an answer back.

He was found at 2 a.m. at about the 6,000-foot level in Paradise Park, west of Zig Zag Canyon. He does not recall the rescuers finding him. In a state of severe hypothermia, he had removed much of his clothing (a phenomenon known as "paradoxical undressing"). He was given a high-calorie paste and hot liquid, along with warm clothing and a bivy bag, and the team built snow walls to block the wind.

The patient was unable to walk, and a helicopter evacuation was unlikely due to intermittent whiteout conditions and a projected 2.5-hour wait for the flight crew. The decision was made to drag a litter carrying the patient about 3,700 vertical feet down to the road. Additional rescuers from various teams made their way to the party to assist, and everyone finally made it to the Paradise Park trailhead at 2 p.m. on Saturday, 12 hours after the initial contact. The snowboarder was transferred to a waiting ambulance, which took him to Mountain Medical, where he was rewarmed and treated with IV fluids.

ANALYSIS
Getting an early start (often before daybreak) is usually necessary to complete a successful climb of Mt. Hood. Sticking to his original timeline and plan for not pursuing a summit, this climber may have avoided this incident. Carrying a compass or fully charged GPS and preprogrammed coordinates could have helped him find his way down to Timberline Lodge, even in whiteout conditions. He also had inadequate clothing, food, and water to survive an unexpected night out. However, the patient did well to stop and seek shelter and to call 911 before his phone died, thus giving rescuers his location coordinates. These decisions undoubtedly saved his life. (*Sources: Portland Mountain Rescue, news reports, and climber's Facebook post.*)

AVALANCHE
Mt. Hood, Leuthold Couloir

On May 23 at approximately 12:30 p.m., search and rescue coordinators were notified of an injured climber who had been in an avalanche. In the early morning hours of May 23, Danielle (23) and Shelby (28) set out to climb the Leuthold Couloir, on the west side of Mt. Hood, above the Reid Glacier.

Danielle was approximately 10 to 15 feet above Shelby when an avalanche was triggered just above the Hourglass, a narrowing in the couloir. She tried arresting her slide but was pulled under. Shelby tried to grab her as she passed, but could not reach her. He noted her location and then, seconds later, a second slide swept him down the couloir.

Danielle was carried approximately 1,000 feet down onto the Reid Glacier. Shelby was able to arrest his slide earlier, and he scrambled down the debris path to Danielle and assessed her condition. The climbers sent a distress call by inReach around noon. Somewhat miraculously, neither was seriously injured, though Danielle had an ankle injury.

The climbers' location and responders' fatigue immediately following an all-night response to a stranded snowboarder (*see report above*) made for a difficult rescue, involving multiple teams. Upon reaching the climbers, one group of rescuers treated Danielle and packaged her in a SKED litter, and another set up a line to haul her more than 500 vertical feet to Illumination Saddle, from which they would be able to ski down with her to Timberline Lodge. The climbers and rescue teams reached Timberline at 9:30 p.m. Danielle chose to seek her own medical attention.

ANALYSIS
The climbers were well equipped, with avalanche safety gear and cell phones and a Garmin inReach for emergency communications. There are no formal avalanche forecasts for Mt. Hood this late in the season, but alerts had been posted on social

media that avalanche risk would be high, following significant recent snowfall over an icy layer and warming temperatures.

Between the two operations over Memorial Day Weekend, search and rescue teams worked on Mt. Hood for nearly 23 hours straight. (*Source: Clackamas County Sheriff's Office and news reports.*)

LONG SKIING FALL INTO FUMAROLE
Mt. Hood, South Side

On June 18, Scott Miller, a 25-year-old skier from Utah, missed a turn while descending from the summit and took a long fall that ended in a fumarole below. He had planned to ski Mt. Hood and Mt. Shasta en route to a job posting in Northern California. After a rapid climb to the summit via the Pearly Gates, Miller chose Old Chute for his descent. It looked steep and he could feel the snow was hardpacked, but it seemed within his ability.

After starting down by side-slipping, he launched a jump turn but lost his edges on the icy snow and began to slide. Miller slid and tumbled down the chute, hitting some rocks, and fell into an open fumarole, a crevasse-like opening in the snow and ice through which volcanic gases emerge.

Luckily, onlookers had seen his fall and ran over to the fumarole from the Hogsback. One of these was Win Van Pelt, who had witnessed the skier flying down toward the fumarole. Van Pelt yelled down and was able to confirm Miller was alive and able to move. The skier tried to climb out of the fumarole, but slipped and dropped in even further. Van Pelt confirmed the skier was carrying a harness and asked him to put it on, and then he and his partner rigged a 3:1 haul system and extracted him.

Very fortunately, Miller had only minor injuries, and after assessment he was able to put on his crampons and walk down the mountain with Van Pelt and his partner accompanying him.

ANALYSIS
Miller wrote: "It's a big step to the more advanced lines on the volcanoes. Don't underestimate a slope looking down from the top, and don't overestimate your ability to ski something just because you've been around [similar slopes] before in controlled environments. Had I spent more time researching, I would have known this [part of the] mountain doesn't get enough sun to ski until late afternoon," when the snow surface softens. "In summary, I got lucky.... I'm an inexperienced climber with a lot to learn still. I got lucky my inexperience didn't get me severely hurt or get me killed." (*Sources: Reports by Scott Miller and Win Van Pelt. Miller was interviewed about this incident for Episode 61 of the Sharp End Podcast.*)

SKI FATALITY ON MT. HOOD: *On February 25, an experienced 47-year-old mountaineer was skiing alone in the Illumination Saddle area after summiting Mt. Hood, and was discovered around noon after an apparent fall. He succumbed to his injuries. The skiing conditions on the mountain were difficult and dangerous at the time, with very large ice "chickenhead" formations covering the slopes.*

FALL ON ICE | Insufficient Footwear
Mt. Hood, South Side

At 9:42 a.m. on Sunday, July 26, the Clackamas County Sheriff's Office was notified of an accident on Mt. Hood. A married couple (both in their early 30s) had fallen about 700 feet (initially reported as 1,000 feet) and had suffered injuries.

Other climbers on the mountain made their way to where the two had fallen and rendered aid. Their location was determined to be west of the Hogsback, behind Crater Rock, at approximately 10,000 feet, having come to rest near the Hot Rocks fumarole. Various agencies responded, and a team of rescuers reached the climbers just after 1 p.m. Rescuers stabilized the woman, who was more seriously injured, and began the decent to Timberline Lodge, arriving at around 6 p.m. She was transported to a hospital for treatment of non-life-threatening injuries.

ANALYSIS
These climbers were wearing micro-spikes instead of technical crampons. MICRO-spikes, Yaktrax, and similar traction devices for trail runners are being spotted more frequently on the mountain, but they are not safe to use; appropriate crampons and boots are necessary in all conditions on Mt. Hood. Rescue coordinators also stressed in their post-accident notes that July 26 is late for climbing Mt. Hood, and that conditions are more difficult and dangerous in late summer, including increased falling ice and rockfall.

The climbers were roped together but were not setting protection to hold a fall. Depending on the team's experience, the angle of the slope, and the snow conditions, a team that ropes up to protect against falls (versus crevasses) should strongly consider running belays using pickets or ice screws for protection. (*Sources: Clackamas County Sheriff's Office and Portland Mountain Rescue.*)

FATAL FALL INTO CREVASSE | Climbing Alone
Mt. Hood, Eliot Glacier

The body of Austin Mishler, 27, an experienced climber and wilderness guide, was found October 29 in a crevasse at about 9,400 feet on Mt. Hood's north side. The Bend resident likely fell while soloing in technical terrain, and he ended up in a crevasse in the upper Eliot Glacier icefall.

On October 28, Mishler was reported missing by family members. His tent on the Snow Dome was spotted by aerial searchers, and a team from the Hood River Crag Rats reached the tent at 9,000 feet at 2 a.m. on October 29. As multiple teams searched the Eliot and Coe glaciers, family members recalled that Mishler had a SPOT satellite

Recovery team works to haul a climber from dangerous terrain below the Snow Dome on Mt. Hood's north side. *Hood River Crag Rats*

beacon and were able to locate the serial number. The Hood River Sheriff's Office contacted SPOT and learned the unit had been continuously sending data from a single location since October 27. A team responded to the location and found the man's body. A complex all-day recovery mission was completed by volunteers from Portland Mountain Rescue and the Crag Rats several days later.

ANALYSIS

According to mission leader Christopher Van Tilburg of Hood River Crag Rats, the fatality was likely due to an unroped solo fall from the area of Anderson Rock, roughly 500 vertical feet above where the body was found. Always let someone know where you are headed, especially if you are venturing out on a highly technical solo adventure. If you use a satellite locator device, make sure a responsible party knows which brand you are using. In this case, the SPOT device had been continuously transmitting the person's location, and if rescuers had learned this sooner, they would have reached the victim earlier and exposed themselves to less risk. (*Sources: Christopher Van Tilburg, Hood River Crag Rats, and news reports.*)

Site of climber's fall into a hidden fumarole. *Courtesy of Clackmas County Sheriff's Office*

FALL INTO HIDDEN FUMAROLE
Mt. Hood, South Side

On December 4, a climber, Caroline Sundbaum, 32, of Portland, fell 15 feet into a fumarole on Mt. Hood, injuring her shoulder. Sundbaum, whose two climbing partners had continued up the mountain ahead of her, had sat on her pack to rest at the top of the White River Glacier canyon, downslope from Devil's Kitchen, at approximately 11,200 feet. Another climber saw her sit down. A few moments later, when he looked back, she had disappeared.

The climber realized there was a hole in the snow where Sundbaum had been sitting, called 911, and made his way over to the fumarole. He lowered a rope to Sundbaum, and she was was able to secure herself with the rope and be hoisted out to safety.

A member of Portland Mountain Rescue (PMR) happened to be on Mt. Hood at the time and headed toward the scene to assist, as did Sundbaum's two climbing partners, who had learned about the accident. Sundbaum injured her shoulder, but with help she was able to make her way to the top of the Palmer lift, where a Sno-Cat picked her up for transport down the mountain.

ANALYSIS

Very fortunately, another climber witnessed this incident—it would have been extremely difficult to locate Sundbaum otherwise, since her party had separated.

The air inside fumaroles can be toxic and potentially deadly. Mt. Hood is an active volcano and hot gases from fumaroles create large hidden cavities, ranging from a few feet to 20 feet high. These holes may be hidden by a blanket of snow, and a climber can easily break through the roof of these cavities, where gases may collect in deadly concentrations.

Fumarole cavities form in the same general areas every year—the most familiar are Hot Rocks and Devil's Kitchen—and are often revealed by depressions in the snow surface or open holes in the snow. If you do not know where the fumarole areas are, ask knowledgeable climbers. Know before you go. (*Sources: Clackamas County Sheriff's Office and Portland Mountain Rescue.*)

FALL ON SNOW/ICE
Mt. Jefferson

On July 25, an experienced climber from Kennewick, Washington, slipped and fell to his death while traversing a glacier high on the slopes of 10,495-foot Mt. Jefferson (likely on the Whitewater Glacier route). David Freepons, 68, who had decades of mountaineering experience, fell on the east side of the mountain at about 9,500 feet and hit a rocky outcrop during his slide. Freepons was found deceased by his three fellow climbers about 600 feet downhill from the site of his fall.

ANALYSIS
According to one member of the climber's team, Freepons was her climbing mentor and a leader in her mountaineering community. She said the group was properly equipped and had taken appropriate safety precautions. (*Source: Jefferson County Sheriff's Office and news reports.*)

RAPPEL ERROR | Uneven Rope, Inadequate Backup
Smith Rock State Park

A group of three was climbing Wherever I May Roam (5.9), a popular multi-pitch sport route, on the afternoon of August 8, and they decided to rappel before completing the climb. The team reportedly did not find the middle of their rope and tied a stopper knot only in one end of the rope.

One of the climbers (male, 22) began to rappel and then fell to the ground after the short, unknotted end of the rope passed through his device. He fell approximately 90 feet to the ground, then tumbled another 150 feet down a steep slope, coming to rest near the Misery Ridge Trail. He took the rope with him as he fell, stranding the two partners.

People nearby ran to help and called 911. The injured climber reportedly was awake and communicating. Two volunteers headed up the route to help the remaining two climbers in the party off the wall.

Redmond Fire & Rescue and Deschutes County SAR team members used a raft to cross the Crooked River and reach the climber. He was treated, prepped, then floated across the river to a waiting helicopter that flew him to the hospital. The injured climber had a broken hip and collapsed lung.

ANALYSIS

The same safety steps should be followed for every single rappel, whether a single rap or a long series of rappels down a big face: Make sure the two rope ends are even (if you can't see them, gather the ends at the stance so you can lower them simultaneously), knot both ends, use a friction-hitch backup, and weight-test the system before unclipping from the anchor and committing to the rappel. These steps would prevent a very large majority of serious rappel accidents. (*Sources: Deschutes County Search and Rescue, news reports, and Mountain Project.*)

FALL ON ROCK | Inadequate Belay, Inexperience
Smith Rock State Park

On December 27, 2019, I took a long fall while attempting a sport climb at the southern tip of the Smith Rock Group, belayed by my father, who had no outdoor climbing experience. My parents were visiting me in Bend for the holidays, and we had gone to Smith to check out the park and get in some climbing. My wife, who, like me, is an experienced climber, was not available that day, so I decided to have my father belay, figuring a Grigri would lock in a lead-fall situation. I gave my father, who was a complete novice as a belayer, a quick overview of how to use a Grigri 2. I warmed up on one route, then set up a top-rope on a harder adjacent route. On the harder route, I hung on the top-rope several times to demonstrate to my father how to hold me with the Grigri.

Figuring he had belaying down, I decided to work on another sport route I had tried once before, but wasn't able to do clean: I'm Your Hate (5.11a). I started up the route on lead and asked my father to take several times as I proceeded toward the crux. I started into the crux section, which involves coming out of a dihedral and around an arête, and then fell. I was only a few feet above a bolt, but I dropped approximately 35 feet to the ground.

I landed on both feet with the rope taut, implying the Grigri had caught my weight just as or before I hit the ground. We believe my father mistakenly held open the release mechanism on the Grigri with one hand as he attempted to arrest my fall. The Grigri eventually engaged, likely when my father experienced a minor rope burn on his hand and thus released his grip.

Using a pair of crutches kept at the park for community use, I was able to self-rescue. I later learned I had fractured my right calcaneus (heel bone) in the incident, which required surgical repair.

ANALYSIS

I was so excited to go climbing and, lacking an experienced partner, I decided to recruit an inexperienced belayer. I assumed the Grigri would prevent a leader fall no matter what. However, like all belay devices, the Grigri requires proper training and experience to use effectively. I should have put more focus on belay training and practice, and stuck with climbs well within my onsight capabilities. (*Source: Tom Bussell, age 36.*) [*Editor's Note: Since this incident occurred in late 2019, it is not counted in the data tables. We included it here as a useful reminder that assisted-braking belay devices are never foolproof. Provide or seek sufficient instruction and follow the manufacturer's recommendations when using any new or unfamiliar device.*]

UTAH

GROUND FALL | Loose Rock Severs Rope
Wasatch Range, Big Cottonwood Canyon, Whipple Fork

On April 8, Wade Joseph Meade, 29, an experienced climber, and his partner, Tyler Grundstrom, who has been climbing about 10 years and is also an EMT, had decided to explore the Whipple Fork area, high in Big Cottonwood Canyon, for first-ascent potential. Just reaching the base requires an hour-plus scramble up "the nastiest talus and bushwhacking you can imagine," Grundstrom said. One reason they had sought a remote area was to avoid COVID exposure.

Once in the area, the pair assessed two potential climbs. At the base of one of these, Meade tied in and started leading up a hand and fist crack. When Meade was about 50 feet up, he pulled off a quartzite flake about 3 feet by 1.5 feet by 1 foot. As he was falling, the flake cut the rope. He landed on the belay ledge and then tumbled 25 more feet, bouncing over rocks and coming to rest at the bottom of the approach couloir on a patch of snow.

Grundstrom immediately climbed down to his friend and completed a full assessment, and within a couple of minutes called the police to initiate a rescue. Meade, who was wearing a helmet, had several apparent injuries: an open fracture of his right elbow, to which Grundstrom later applied a tourniquet to control the bleeding; a chest injury that led Grundstrom to believe Meade had a collapsed lung; a possible right orbital fracture around the eye; deformation of his lower lumbar spine, with no sensation or motor movement in his legs; and a pelvic fracture. He was conscious but disoriented, and Grundstrom believed he might have a traumatic brain injury.

Grundstrom built a platform of backpacks to allow Meade to lie on top of the snow, piled layers on him for warmth, and got him into a better position for breathing. Rescuers from various agencies arrived at the scene approximately 1.5 to 2 hours after Grundstrom called 911, and they prepared for a difficult helicopter hoist to extract the patient. As he was being transported off the mountain, about 5:35 p.m., Meade succumbed to his injuries.

ANALYSIS
The subject was an experienced climber who suffered a tragic accident. According to Grundstrom, this was Meade's first attempt at establishing a new route, and the two had agreed on a strict ground-up ethic. As a result, they chose not to rappel the line and remove loose rocks before climbing. (*Sources: Tyler Grundstrom, Rock and Ice, Salt Lake County Search and Rescue.*)

STRANDED | Unable to Pull Rappel Rope
Wasatch Range, Big Cottonwood Canyon

Salt Lake County Search and Rescue was called out at 12:30 a.m. on July 16 for a pair of climbers (father and son) who had been stranded while trying to descend from a multi-pitch route near Steort's Ridge. Their rappel rope had gotten stuck, and when they were unable to free it, they eventually called 911 for help.

When rescuers responded, they determined the best way to reach them would be from below, and since dawn was not far off, the climbers were asked to wait for morning light. Two rescuers then climbed to the pair and helped them rappel to the bottom. (*Source: Salt Lake County Search and Rescue.*)

ANALYSIS

It's not known what caused the climbers' rope to get stuck or how they tried to free it. (A similar incident at this cliff was reported in ANAC 2019.) However, one takeaway is that climbers should be prepared with extra clothing layers, food, and water. This pair wore shorts and unexpectedly spent all night perched on a small ledge. (*Source: The Editors.*)

BELAYER HIT BY ROCKFALL | Saved by Borrowed Helmet
Wasatch Range, Little Cottonwood Canyon, Hellgate Cliffs

Using a rope bag as a makeshift litter for a short, steep carry to a helicopter landing zone. *Salt Lake County Search and Rescue*

On August 7, Avery Guest (female, 20) was climbing with her partner for the day, Jake Bowles (21), at Hellgate Cliffs, a limestone area high in Little Cottonwood. It was Avery's second time climbing/belaying outdoors. Jake is an experienced climber.

They chose Monkey Paw (5.9), a single-pitch sport climb, for their first route of the day. Jake was leading, and he got about four bolts up the route (approximately 50 feet off the ground) when he reached for what looked like a good hold. When he weighted the hold, a torso-size rock detached from the wall. It split into three pieces, and one of them landed on Avery, knocking her unconscious. Jake fell approximately 10 feet, pulling Avery about a foot off the ground. She was using a Grigri, which caught Jake's fall.

Avery regained consciousness quickly and noticed she had an open fracture on her right arm. She managed to lower her partner with her left hand, and he untied her from the belay system. She had post-traumatic amnesia, repeating questions multiple times. They called 911 at about 10:20 a.m. United Fire Authority paramedics and Salt Lake County Search and Rescue responded to the scene within 30 minutes. They gave her pain medication and improvised a litter with Jake's rope bag in order to carry her about 100 feet down and away from the base of the rock, where Lifeflight could hoist Avery and transport her to the hospital for treatment.

She had two broken bones in her right arm that needed surgery, plus lacerations on her forehead and leg. She also had bleeding in her brain, but managed to avoid brain surgery. Jake suffered only minor scrapes and bruises during the fall.

ANALYSIS

Avery did not have a helmet, so Jake let her use his, knowing there might be rockfall in the area. If Avery had not been wearing Jake's helmet, her head injuries could have been much worse and possibly fatal. The belay stance for this route was small and surrounded by steep, rocky slopes. Otherwise, she may have been able to move out of the way of the falling rock. (*Source: Avery Guest.*)

Editor's Note: Although such incidents are thankfully rare, this is an excellent example of a case where an assisted-braking belay device likely prevented serious injuries to the leader, because the belayer's device stopped his fall even though the belayer had been knocked unconscious by rockfall.

LEADER FALLS | Cams Pulled Out
Wasatch Range, Little Cottonwood Canyon

Salt Lake County Search and Rescue (SLCOSAR) was called out in the afternoon of October 19 for an injured climber in Little Cottonwood Canyon. The very experienced climber (male, 59) had been leading the first pitch of Crescent Crack (5.7 trad) when he took a lead fall and a cam placement failed to hold. The climber dropped about 25 feet and flipped upside down with the rope caught behind his leg. He landed head-first on a ledge (he credits his helmet with saving his life). The belayer, his 20-year-old son, lowered the injured climber to a ledge, where he shakily slung a tree for another anchor (nearly dropping the rope in the process), and then was lowered to the ground.

The climber later wrote: "I had already placed much of the gear on my rack in the crack below me and lacked the size I needed to protect the next move. I reached down, grabbed my last cam, and bumped it up higher—keenly aware that the next piece below that one was now more than 10 feet down. I reset the cam a few times. It wasn't the ideal size for the crack, but I believed I finally set it securely. [This was] possibly the first time in 30 years of climbing that a piece of gear I'd placed didn't hold when I fell on it."

The leader was evacuated to the hospital, where scans revealed fractured C1 and T3 vertebrae and a massive contusion on one thigh. Fortunately, he recovered completely from the serious spinal injuries.

The day after the Crescent Crack incident, SLCOSAR was called for another injured climber in Little Cottonwood. A climber was leading Bongeater (5.10d trad) when he fell at the crux near the top of the route. His climbing partner said he fell about six to ten feet to the last cam placement below him, and that cam pulled out. The next two cams below that also pulled out. The fourth piece of gear held, but the climber hit a ramp. Two broken ankles were suspected. The climber also had the rope briefly wrapped around his neck in the fall, causing ligature marks. The belayer lowered the climber and called for help. Unified Fire and SLCOSAR brought the patient to the trailhead, from which he was transported to a local hospital. (*Sources: Salt Lake County Search and Rescue and climber account.*)

ANALYSIS

In the first accident, a cam placement failed; in the second, multiple placements failed. The first climber knew his final cam placement was poor but continued anyway. He wrote: "I've castigated myself ad nauseam over my decision to continue upward instead of lowering to a ledge where I could have built an anchor, belayed my son up, and had the full rack to finish the pitch. I may have misled myself, in part, because the difficulty rating of that pitch was relatively easy—a grade on which I'm not sure I've ever fallen before. Despite all the good reasons to back off, I convinced myself: *It'll be fine.*"

On Bongeater, the crux is a layback crack that can be protected well with cams, but on such strenuous moves it's common to skip or rush placements; the result in this case was three cams pulling out. (*Source: The Editors.*)

FALL ON ROCK | Dislodged Block, Inadequate Protection
Wasatch Range, Pfeifferhorn, North Ridge

On November 6, my partner (male, 25) and I, John Sigmon (32), set out to attempt the north ridge of Pfeifferhorn before a storm came in and potentially snowed out the route. It was both of our first times on this climb, and we were aware of reports of loose rock in the summer and fall, especially in the upper sections of the route. A short while after gaining the ridge, we decided to rope up and simul-climb due to loose rock and a few exposed sections. I was leading about two-thirds of the way up the 800-foot ridge, with one cam between me and my partner. After walking across a horizontal area full of small ledges and loose rock, there were two low-angle corners in front of me. The left one looked easier, if a little loose, with an obvious opportunity for protection at the bottom. The right one looked harder but a little more fun, with obvious protection about 15 feet up.

Accident site on the north ridge of Pfeifferhorn. The climbers self-rescued over the top and down the trail to their car. *John Sigmon Collection*

I started up the right corner and spotted a nice stance on a three-foot-wide ledge above me, where I expected to place a piece. The ledge looked solid. I pulled up with both hands to mantel, with my feet smearing, when suddenly the top foot or so of the ledge broke off. I fell and hit the ledge below, thinking I would stop, but then kept rolling. I yelled out "falling!" and bounced again, then came to a stop on another ledge. The rope never came tight due to the distance to my last piece.

I immediately sat up and moved all my hands and feet, visually checking my extremities for unusual angles. I noticed pain in my right elbow, right hip, and left ankle. My fingertips tingled for several minutes. I yelled for my partner to come up and help, and he assisted in removing my shoe and checking my ankle, which hurt and was swollen but had good range of motion. Nothing seemed broken and I didn't seem to have any head, neck, or spine injuries. With only a few hundred feet to the summit, and most of the fifth class behind us, we decided the fastest way out was up.

My partner led the remaining sections until we hit easy terrain and unroped. We descended the third-class terrain from the summit and then headed out via the hiking trail for approximately a 5.5-mile trip back to the car.

ANALYSIS

Knowing the route was 5.4 and full of loose rock, I should have followed the easiest line and been diligent about placing more protection. The rock that came off looked so well-attached that I didn't even bother to tap on it. In the future, I will test critical holds more carefully. I consider myself lucky. I ended up with two weeks of rest for a minor ankle sprain and some contusions, and was climbing again a few weeks later, although with a little less courage than before. (*Source: John Sigmon.*)

Editor's Note: These climbers used a 30-meter rope, a good tactic for simul-climbing. A short (or shortened) rope improves communication and reduces rope drag, allowing more protection to be placed; long slings also ease rope drag while simul-climbing.

HIT BY FALLING ICE NEAR BASE OF CLIMB
Wasatch Range, Provo Canyon

Around 10:30 a.m. on January 12, a group of three climbers arrived at the base of the Stairway to Heaven (WI5) in Provo Canyon. The first pitch of this long climb is about 190 feet long, with a ledge system that bisects the pitch a bit less than halfway up. This ledge can be accessed without lead climbing by hiking uphill to climber's right and then traversing the ledge system. A couple of bolted anchors adorn this ledge, as well as the opportunity to build anchors with ice screws. The ice below is called the Apron (WI3) and is a popular top-roping venue. On a busy weekend, the Apron may accommodate up to a dozen ropes on lines from 30 feet to about 80 feet.

The Apron is located atop a rocky and snowy gully that gains approximately 300 feet at an average angle of 35–40 degrees. Particularly large or severe icefall or rock-fall occasionally enters the upper reaches of this gully, but avalanches are rare due to the low elevation and limited snow accumulation. The Apron itself is also subject to icefall, typically from the climbing parties that accumulate there or from the upper pitches of Stairway to Heaven.

On this day, Persons 1 and 3 waited below the Apron while Person 2 hiked up to the ledge and traversed across to set up a top-rope. Persons 1 and 3 were located away from the base of the ice, so they would be unlikely to be hit by climber-generated icefall from parties on the Apron. Person 2 had just finished rigging a top-rope when a large chunk of ice (witnesses estimate approximately 12 inches in diameter) fell from above Person 2. The ice fell unimpeded for more than 150 feet and struck Person 1 on the top of the head.

Person 1 was wearing a helmet but was immediately rendered unresponsive from the impact and fell over backward. Rigid and still unconscious, the individual

began to slide head-first on their back down the approach gully, narrowly missing vegetation and larger rocks. Person 3 and I (who was teaching nearby) gave chase as Person 1 slid down the gully. Person 3 nearly reached Person 1 and then leapt face-first downhill in an effort to stop Person 1, in a manner that can only be described as heroic. Person 3 wrapped their arms around Person 1's legs and both slid downhill together for a few more feet. At that point, I had advanced downhill and was able to fully stop both of them by supporting Person 1's shoulders. Person 1 had slid approximately 150 feet downhill before being stopped.

Within moments, Person 1 regained responsiveness. Other climbers came to help, including Person 2, who had rappelled, and North Fork Fire Rescue and Utah County Sheriff Search and Rescue arrived on scene within approximately 20 minutes. They assumed medical care of Person 1 and executed a semi-technical litter evacuation down the approach gully. Person 1 suffered a concussion and whiplash but no other injuries.

Stairway to Heaven in Provo Canyon. The Apron area (circled) is at the base of the five-pitch climb. *John Ross*

ANALYSIS

Falling ice is quite common at the Apron, as there are often parties with beginners who may not be skilled at avoiding displacement of ice while climbing. However, this icefall is relatively predictable and benign, mitigated by appropriate positioning of the belayer and other party members.

Natural icefall and occasional rockfall are less predictable. The fifth pitch of Stairway to Heaven, about 350 feet above the Apron, is a pillar that begins as a hanging dagger. If the temperature warms above freezing, the lower-angle ice flows of the first three pitches of Stairway to Heaven (including the Apron) may remain climbable, but the fifth pitch may suddenly fall off, showering the whole area with large chunks of ice. Consequently, before choosing to climb here, the wary climber checks conditions (there is a weather station at the trailhead), the forecast for the elevation of the upper climb, and the visual appearance of the fifth-pitch pillar to determine if there's a likelihood the fifth pitch might collapse.

On the day of this accident, the temperature at the trailhead did not rise above freezing, with moderate wind and some snowfall at the Apron in the early to midmorning.

It is not unusual for parties to top-rope on the Apron when there are climbers above on the higher pitches of Stairway of Heaven. Nonetheless, this increases the overhead hazard, as icefall may be generated from climbers well above the Apron. (Parties rappelling may also dislodge rocks or ice blocks, particularly when pulling ropes; multi-pitch parties should consider walking off to climber's right from the base of pitch two.) In this case, it appears the icefall may have come from a party on the upper part of pitch two on Stairway or the lower part of pitch three. Stairway to Heaven is characterized by expansive ledges separating relatively vertical pitches of ice. Often, the ledges are snow-covered and are of sufficient size that icefall will stop at the ledge below. However, in early season or lean snow years, there may be insufficient snow on the ledges for this to be reliable.

Given Person 1's conservative positioning in a relatively protected area, away from the base of the route, it is difficult to ascribe the icefall impact to much other than inherent risk and bad luck. From an outside perspective, their positioning seemed appropriate. It's likely this accident only could have been prevented if parties elected not to climb the Apron with others above or if multi-pitch parties elected not to begin the upper pitches with parties already established on the Apron below. (*Source: Derek DeBruin.*)

GROUND FALL BEFORE FIRST BOLT | Fatigue
Moab Area, Potash Road, Mars Wall

On June 23, my friend and I went to Mars Wall to do a few after-work pitches. I had taught her how to lead belay and taken some short practice falls with her a few weeks earlier. I (female, 28) had not been climbing very much in the months leading up to the accident, and although I previously sport climbed regularly, I had been climbing primarily trad and wasn't in the habit of bringing a stick clip.

I first led a bolted 5.9+ that I had done the year before. It felt hard but within my ability, and I did it with no takes or falls. The light was fading faster than I would have hoped, but I decided to try the route next door, Tax Free $ (5.10c), also a sport climb. I felt this route would be within my ability, though a challenge.

The base of the climb was uneven and sloping away from the wall. There was a large, fallen tree at the base with roots that jut up toward the climb. My belayer offered to spot me, but I declined because it seemed like an awkward place and perhaps dangerous for her. The start felt insecure, and I fell off twice, about five feet off the ground, before clipping the first bolt.

I decided to push myself and give it one more try. I slipped and again fell approximately five feet, this time landing awkwardly on my left ankle before somersaulting backward down the slope. The rope came tight around the fallen tree and arrested my fall. Immediately I knew that my left ankle was hurt. Otherwise, I had only a few scrapes. The helmet I was wearing likely prevented a minor concussion from the rocky slope. After visiting the hospital, I learned I had a slight calcaneus fracture and had shattered the horn of my talus bone.

ANALYSIS
The contributing factors to this accident were lack of fitness, fatigue, and inadequate equipment. A wet winter, social distancing, and three jobs prevented me from climbing in the months leading up to the accident, and I overestimated my fitness. When I started to lead this pitch, it was late in the day and I was tired. If I had brought and used a stick clip, I would have been protected before the first bolt. [*Editor's Note:*

Although not practical on this route, it's often possible to preclip the first or second bolt of a difficult climb by climbing and lowering from an adjacent route.] (Source: Kate Weigel.)

STRANDED | Incorrect Anchor, Stuck Rappel Ropes
Castle Valley, Castleton Tower, West Face

Just after sunset on December 4, two male climbers (ages 32 and 36) called 911 to report they were stranded halfway down 400-foot Castleton Tower because their rappel ropes had become stuck. Starting near sunrise, the pair had climbed the Kor-Ingalls Route (5.9) on the tower's south side. They topped out later than expected, with about an hour and a half of daylight left.

Armed with guidebook photos and online beta, they planned to descend via the standard North Face rappels. The two saw a beefy new anchor on top of the north-west corner of the tower and decided this must be the first rappel anchor. Tying two 70-meter ropes together, the first rappeler descended about 200 feet and spotted a bolted anchor 25 feet to his right, but no other suitable anchor before the ends of the ropes. No longer in voice contact with his partner, he ascended a short distance and moved right to reach the bolted anchor. It appeared that one more double-rope rappel would get them to the ground. Once both climbers reached the mid-face anchor, they attempted to pull the ropes. Despite applying full body weight to the pull line, they could not get the ropes to budge.

Contemplating ascending the stuck rope, the climbers realized the other strand had swung out of reach across a blank face. The climbers agreed that recovering the other strand was not safe or practical, nor was climbing the unknown chimney above them in the dark. The climbers were aware the temperature was expected to drop to 15°F overnight, so they made the call for a rescue. They were prepared with a headlamp, warm jackets, handwarmers, and an emergency bivy sack.

A team of three rescuers from Grand County Search and Rescue was transported to the summit via helicopter. One rescuer rappelled to the subjects around 9 p.m. and assisted them in rappelling to the base of the tower.

ANALYSIS

The rescuers discovered the climbers had mistakenly rappelled from an anchor used to rig a 500-meter highline (slackline) to the neighboring Rectory formation. Instead of rappelling the North Face, as planned, the climbers had ended up on the less-traveled West Face route (5.11). Because the highline anchors were not intended for rappelling, friction made it impossible for the climbers to pull their ropes.

The climbing party identified a number of decisions that could have prevented this misadventure. Had they abandoned the climb and rappelled the Kor-Ingalls Route earlier, they probably would have been down before sunset. Even after finishing the route, heading back down the Kor-Ingalls would have had the advantage of familiarity with the anchor stations, rather than rappelling into unknown territory. Lastly, while the highline anchor is quite visible atop the tower, its configuration, set back from the cliff edge with very short chain links, indicates it is not appropriate for a rappel. The climbers may have felt rushed with the setting sun and dropping temperature, but if they had looked more thoroughly, they likely would have found the North Face rappel station, about 30 feet away on top of the tower. This anchor's bolts have three or four feet of chain that extend over the edge and attach to large rappel rings, making for an easy pull.

After word got out about these stranded climbers, a local guide removed the chain links from the highline anchor to discourage future incidents. (The links can easily be reinstalled to rig the highline.) There is a plan to attach plaques identifying the bolts as a highline anchor. (*Sources: The climbers, Grand County SAR, and the Editors.*)

EDITOR'S NOTE: *It is common for minor mishaps to cascade into a call for rescue. Had the climbers noticed they did not seem to be rappelling in the correct place, they might have been more cautious about maintaining control of both ends of the rappel ropes. A test pull after the first climber descended also could have revealed the problem, allowing the upper climber to extend the anchor with slings or the lower climber to ascend the ropes and return to the top. Once a rope gets stuck at an anchor above, climbers can decide whether to ascend the rope, lead climb up to the anchor, cut the rope and descend with the remaining rope, or call for help. The last option may have been the only one left for these climbers to get off the tower safely.*

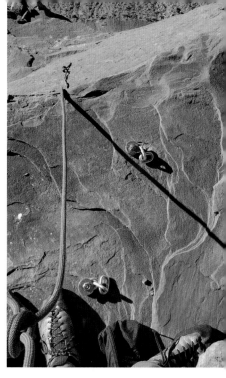

Bolts installed to anchor a highline atop the northwest corner of Castleton Tower, Utah. The correct rappel station is about 30 feet to the right.

As highlines, BASE jumps, and space nets grow in popularity, the number of nonclimbing bolted anchors at cliffs is on the rise, and rescues like this one are becoming more prevalent. In fact, this is the second stranding resulting from an attempted rappel off this same highline anchor in five years. Study the published descriptions of anchor locations, and be aware that guidebooks and online references may not list nonclimbing anchors. If an anchor does not appear to be rigged properly for rappelling—especially on a very popular formation like Castleton Tower—look around and consider the options before committing to the rappel.

LOWERING ERROR | Rope Too Short, No Stopper Knot
Moab Area, Lower Dakota Crag

My climbing partner and I went to the Dakota Crags in the La Sal Mountains on October 21. It was a beautiful day for climbing, and we wanted to begin on some easy routes. We looked at the guidebook as well as a phone app to determine which routes we were looking at. However, additional climbs had been put up since either information source was updated, so I ended up climbing a different route than expected.

The route, Good Times (5.7), was very pleasing. It is a very long route, about 115 feet (35 meters), and my partner's rope is only 60 meters. After I finished the route, I lowered and cleaned the draws. After I took off the second-to-last draw, I heard him curse and then I began to fall.

I fell about 30 feet to the ground, hit a ledge, which broke both of my heels, and then landed on my bum, which broke my tailbone. I then fell back and hit my head on a sharp boulder, as well as my left arm. Luckily, I was wearing a helmet.

It was 3 p.m. and sundown was close to 7 p.m., so we had about four hours to get out. I tried to stand, but I couldn't, and then tried limping with a sturdy stick. I was unable to weight my feet, so I began to crawl. It took me two hours of crawling to reach the truck. Then we had another 45 minutes of driving on bumpy dirt roads back to Moab. Finally, I headed to the hospital. (*Source: Kimberly Kelly.*)

ANALYSIS

The climbers misidentified the route they were on and did not know the route requires a 70-meter rope, which is common for this area. Tying in the second climber or tying a stopper knot in the end of the rope would have prevented the climber from hitting the ground. (*Source: The Editors.*)

VERMONT

FALL ON ICE | Collapsed Ice Curtain
Bone Mountain

We were climbing at a remote location in the hills of Bolton, in search of new ice lines. Bone Mountain is an obscure cliff that takes about an hour and a half to reach in summer and about two hours of skinning in the winter. I was very familiar with the area, having developed many of the routes. Two young friends joined me on February 17 to explore for winter lines.

At one of the furthest reaches of the cliff, we saw three distinct ice lines. The largest was a free-standing column around 25 feet tall, and the second was easier. After doing both of these climbs, we looked at a line that began with a free-hanging curtain of ice and talked about how to mitigate the risks. We knew we had a party of three, cell phone reception, and a med kit, and I placed one ice screw uphill from the ice to prevent sliding down the hill if I needed to jump off while leading. The bottom of the ice was roughly two feet from the ground.

The curtain required very slow movement and precision to climb. I ascended the curtain to the point at which it met the rock about 15 feet up, and then, while repositioning one of my tools, the curtain gave way with me on it. I hit the ground and the curtain landed on me, breaking an ankle and lacerating my upper lip. It is unclear if my ankle broke on impact with the ground or from ice landing on it. The lip injury was caused by falling ice.

My partners assessed my injuries and found nothing other than the fractured ankle and lip. I never lost consciousness. We took off my ice boot and put on a ski boot before swelling could occur, mitigated the bleeding from my face, and then proceeded to ski for three-plus hours back to the car. Before leaving, we called a number of friends to give them updates on our situation and then checked in every hour or so on the way down. I was treated for a low tibia/fibula fracture, and the lip required 12 stitches.

ANALYSIS

Simply put, I made a risky call and landed on the wrong side of that call. I knew what I was attempting to climb was dangerous, and ultimately I was either not skilled enough to handle the terrain or I just got unlucky on that day. It's worth noting that the first climb of the day was likely much more dangerous, and a successful lead of that free-standing column may have impacted my decision-making later in the day. This is something I've been reflecting on ever since.

At a more micro level, I was one move away from solid ice when I reached for the ice with my left tool. I felt stretched out and came back down to reposition my right tool. One could argue I should have just completed the initial reach up to good ice. The other wrong call was believing I was above the break line on the curtain—I thought I had reached the point where the ice had bonded to the rock when I was repositioning the tool. In hindsight, this was obviously not true. (*Source: Anonymous climber.*)

LEADER FALL AND HEAD IMPACT

Upper West Bolton

At approximately 1 p.m. on May 28, a 20-year-old male was leading the sport climb Peachy Canoodle (5.9) at Upper West Bolton. My partner, Ben Mirkin, and I were climbing out of sight, but within earshot. The climber fell after clipping the third or fourth bolt. We heard a crashing sound followed by the female belayer shouting to her partner, with no response. She then yelled for help. We lowered off, gathered our first-aid supplies, and went to the scene.

The climber was suspended in the air about 15 feet above the ground and appeared to have taken a 10- to 15-foot fall, possibly after traversing off route. He was conscious, and I communicated with the victim regarding the importance of maintaining spinal alignment. I held the belayer's brake strand as backup, and then she asked us to lower the patient, using the Grigri still clipped to her harness.

Once he was on the ground, Ben and I began to assess the patient. The primary presenting wound was an approximately two-inch laceration of the scalp, likely caused by the helmet's headband. He didn't know if he'd lost consciousness. We assessed his level of orientation, and he correctly identified his name, the date, and the place. We continued with our assessment, with a focus on spinal injury and circulation, sensation, and movement (CSM). A few minutes later, we assessed his orientation again and he could only identify his name. Concerned about intercranial pressure (ICP), we called 911.

Though the patient had potentially lost consciousness during his accident, he reported no spinal pain upon palpation and his CSM was good. We felt that, given the patient's ability to move and the potential ICP issues, it was important to begin evacuation. We tested his orientation again, and he could identify his name and the place, but had trouble with the date. As we exited, we were intercepted by local rescue squads. They took over the evacuation, walking the patient to the trailhead and escorting him onto an ambulance.

ANALYSIS

Although I cannot confirm this, it appears the climber flipped over during the fall. It is very important to monitor the placement of the rope relative to the legs when leading. Although it appears the headband of the helmet caused the climber's laceration, I believe the helmet likely prevented more substantial head trauma. Some other observations:

- Both the climber and the belayer reported they were WFR-certified, and I believe this helped us to more effectively deal with the patient, as he had a good understanding of the need to maintain spinal alignment.
- Always bring a first-aid kit, no matter how "local" and "casual" your day is supposed to be. Check and refresh your first-aid kit periodically. My gloves were old and broke too easily, and my iodine swabs were a bit dry.
- Get some basic training in vertical rescue. In this scenario, because he was conscious and cooperative, it was relatively easy to get the climber back to the ground. This is not always the case. It may be necessary to render first aid on the cliff and assist the victim down. Basic vertical rescue training needs to become the climbing equivalent of AIARE Level 1 in the backcountry skiing world—demand that your partners have it. (*Source: Kel Rossiter, IFMGA mountain guide.*)

WASHINGTON

FALL ON ROCK WHILE WEARING CRAMPONS
North Cascades National Park, North Hozomeen Mountain

On July 4, a 46-year-old male climber attempted a solo climb of North Hozomeen Mountain. At 6:30 p.m., the climber was ascending 3rd- and 4th-class terrain in the south gully when he fell approximately 200 feet down 45-degree rock terrain,

Approximate location of injured climber after a long fall on North Hozomeen. *NPS Photo*

coming to rest in a snow gully at 6,400 feet. The climber chose to stay the night in his location and attempt a self-evacuation in the morning. However, early on July 5, the climber decided he was not able to self-evacuate due to injuries and used an inReach to request a rescue. National Park Service rangers used a helicopter to perform a short-haul extraction of the injured climber. He suffered several broken bones and a head injury.

ANALYSIS
The climber stated the cause of the fall likely was wearing crampons while traveling on rock. He had been wearing cram-

pons for the mostly snow-filled couloir and believed he had only a short section of rock to negotiate, but the terrain remained snow-free longer than expected. Taking the time to stop and remove the crampons likely would have provided more security for him on the rocky terrain. [*Editor's Note: Although many alpine climbers are familiar with climbing rock in crampons, it may feel very awkward and insecure to the less practiced.*]

The climber stated that he doubts he would have survived if he had not been wearing a helmet. He also said his decision-making may have been affected by his head trauma, and that having a climbing partner with him would have helped. (*Sources: North Cascades National Park Mountaineering Rangers and King5.com interview.*)

ROCKFALL | Belayer Injured
North Cascades National Park, Mt. Fury

On July 5, a party of three climbers was attempting a new route on Mt. Fury, a remote peak in the Picket Range. The lead climber accidentally caused some rockfall, which impacted the belayer in the head. Luckily, he was wearing a helmet, but his injuries were such that the party used an inReach device to request a rescue.

ANALYSIS
A first ascent in North Cascades National Park inevitably will involve a fair amount of objective hazards, including rockfall. Whenever possible, choose belay stations that are sheltered or out of the fall line of the leader above. (*Source: North Cascades National Park Mountaineering Rangers.*)

RAPPEL ANCHOR FAILURE | Rock Horn Broke
North Cascades National Park, Mt. Shuksan

On July 19, a party of three climbers was descending Mt. Shuksan after summiting via the Sulphide Glacier route. The party was rappelling the standard descent on Shuksan's summit pyramid. They reached a flat ledge and found an existing anchor consisting of a single loop of red webbing around a rock horn. After pulling the rope from the previous rappel, one of the climbers, a 28-year-old female, began to rig the second-to-last rappel of their descent. She threaded the rope through the anchor, rigged her rappel device, and began to weight the anchor. The rock horn then failed, and the climber fell about 100 feet. The other climbers were not attached to the anchor when the failure occurred. The climber came to rest in 3rd- and 4th-class terrain, suffering an unspecified lower leg injury.

The party activated an inReach device to request a rescue, and the remaining two climbers were able to downclimb to the fallen climber's position and provide basic medical care. At 5:30 p.m., National Park Service rangers arrived on scene via helicopter, and a short-haul operation was performed to extract the injured climber. The rest of the party was able to safely exit the mountain on their own.

ANALYSIS
In an interview with the party, one climber stated they were in a hurry due to the

National Park Service rangers perform a short-haul operation to extract an injured climber from the Shuksan pyramid. *NPS Photo*

lateness of the day and that they were tired from attempting a car-to-car climb of this long route (6,400 feet of elevation gain). The climber said that at this rappel station they did not assess the integrity of the anchor, as they had been doing previously. This decision was influenced by time, fatigue, and the assumption the anchor would be strong, like the other anchors they had used.

When rappelling, it is imperative to assess every anchor before weighting it. Inspect all the slings and other anchor materials, especially the less visible back side of the anchor, to be sure they have not been chewed, weathered, or otherwise damaged. It is not uncommon to encounter structurally unsound rock in the North Cascades; if possible, test anchors with a belay or backup before rappelling, and back up the anchor until the last person in the party descends.

It is possible the horn that failed was not one of the standard descent anchors on Shuksan's summit pyramid. During multi-rappel descents, it is not uncommon to rappel past the standard anchor or to spot an off-route anchor from above and head toward it, thereby missing the optimum anchor. When the descent route is the same as your climbing route, note and remember the position of the standard rappel anchors as you climb. (*Source: North Cascades National Park Mountaineering Rangers.*)

FALL ON ROCK | Unroped Scrambling
North Cascades National Park, Forbidden Peak

On August 14, two climbers were attempting to reach the west ridge of Forbidden Peak via the Cat Scratch Gullies. The two had just switched over to rock shoes and started to travel up a gully unroped when one climber, a 24-year-old male, fell about 60 feet down rocky terrain and into the moat at the base of the gully, sustaining a left lower leg injury.

The climbing partner and a nearby climbing guide assisted the injured climber until National Park Service rangers arrived on scene. Due to the nature of the injury and patient location, a short-haul extraction was performed.

ANALYSIS

This is not the first time an accident has occurred in this area. Climbers attempting this route should be comfortable with route-finding and climbing on 4th-class terrain with limited protection. There are several ways to help prevent falls. Solid movement skills and proper footwear go a long way. In addition, climbers can consider using a running belay or short-pitching in this terrain. (The technique used depends on the climbers' experience and terrain.) When in doubt, while traveling in exposed terrain, consider adding some form of protection. [*Editor's Note: See "Know the Ropes: Safer 4th Class in Accidents 2019.*]

FALLING ICE | Running in Crampons to Escape Debris
North Cascades National Park, Mt. Goode

On September 5, two experienced climbers (female, 32, and male, 36) were attempting to climb the Northeast Buttress of Mt. Goode. A little after 10 a.m., as they were trying to cross from the Goode Glacier onto the start of the rock route, a large piece of ice broke free from the gully above. As chunks of ice began to fall toward the party, the female climber, who was more exposed to the falling ice, ran downhill. During this effort to escape the ice, she caught her crampons on the glacier, stumbled, and fell. She was able to quickly self-arrest and avoided being struck by any of the large chunks of ice. However, due to the fall, the climber injured both ankles (with the crampons likely contributing to the severity of the injury).

The north side of Mt. Goode, above the Goode Glacier. (A) Site of the accident, where ice fell from the gully above as climbers tried to reach the rock buttress. (B) High camp at 5,700 feet. (C) Emergency bivouac and evacuation site at 4,100 feet. *Sean O'Rourke*

The party decided to descend quickly, as they were still exposed to icefall. They made a strong effort to self-evacuate and were able to descend from 5,800 feet to 4,100 feet using a variety of self-rescue techniques. At about 7:30 p.m., the party realized they would not able to descend any further and activated their inReach device to request help. The following morning, National Park Service rangers responded via helicopter, and both climbers were extracted via short-haul.

ANALYSIS
In a post-rescue interview, the climbers stated that their packs weighed about 40 pounds each, which likely contributed to the injuries sustained when the climber fell. (The party was planning a five-day traverse over Goode, Storm King, and Booker Mountain). It was also noted that running in crampons led to the ankle injuries; however, not running could have led to more severe injury due to the falling ice.

The crux of this route is often crossing the Goode Glacier and getting onto the rock, due to the large moat. The party stated they had difficulty finding a reasonable crossing and spent a fair amount of time searching for a route. During this time, they were exposed to overhead hazards. Lastly, the party stated that getting an earlier start (before the temperature warmed) could have mitigated the icefall hazards. (Their departure time was not recorded, but they had camped just below the glacier.) On climbing routes involving snow and ice, the season, temperature, and time of day all may contribute to less safe conditions.

Overall, this party was prepared with the right gear, a communication device, and knowledge of self-rescue techniques, and they made a strong effort to self-evacuate. (*Source: North Cascades National Park Mountaineering Rangers.*)

CREVASSE FALL | Climbing Unroped
Glacier Peak Wilderness, Kololo Peaks

On September 5, Jake Robinson (26) and a partner were traversing below a rock wall near the head of the Suiattle Glacier on Kololo Peaks, at 8,000 feet in elevation. The climbers were unroped, and Jake suddenly plunged into a hidden hole and disappeared. After calling out and getting no response, the partner activated an inReach device. When a search and rescue crew arrived by helicopter, they lowered a team member into the hole, and it was found that Jake had died from injuries in the fall and from drowning.

ANALYSIS
Unseen beneath the snow at this location was a large bergschrund, an ice dome, and a glacial tarn about 20 feet wide and 50 feet below the surface. Although nearby crevasses were visible from the air, the bergschrund was hidden from view in the direction the climbers were traveling, with no indentations or other signs of thin snow. It is not uncommon to cross this low-angle glacier unroped, but crevasses and holes may be found on any glacier in any season. Robinson was very experienced in the Cascades. In June 2019, he became the youngest person to complete the Bulger List of Washington's highest peaks. (*Sources: Snohomish County Sheriff's Office and the Editors.*)

ROCKFALL DURING DESCENT
Morpheus Boulders

On March 21, with COVID-19 shutdowns and social-distancing guidelines in place, my housemate, Will, and I decided to avoid crowded Mt. Saint Helens and instead go search for unclimbed boulders near the established Morpheus area, south of Highway 2 and Skyhomish. I had been climbing outside for about five years at the time of the accident, including multiple climbs in remote areas.

It was a mostly sunny day, with the temperature starting out a bit above freezing and rising steadily. Around midday, we crossed the West Fork Miller River to the north side and decided to head away from the river and up a washout in search of potentially unclimbed rock. There was generally less snow on this south-facing aspect, with only a few patches along our route. After a lot of exploring and a bit of bouldering, the sun began to set, so we decided to pack up and head down the way we'd come.

Will was out in front and I was lagging a safe distance behind, which was fortunate, given what happened next. For context, I weigh more than Will and was also carrying our pads, so I probably had 30 pounds on him. As I got to the steep section in the washout, I turned around to downclimb, placing my hands on a block the size of my torso and stepping down to a smaller block. The foothold broke free when I weighted it, and then the larger block shifted and broke free. I instinctively jumped back, pushing myself to the right of the fall line of the massive block as it careened down the wash. However, it crushed my left hand against the adjacent rock slab as it crashed past.

A moment later, I noticed my pinkie finger dangling, with the middle phalanx displaced and the fingernail hanging by a thread, and the white of the bones in my ring finger showing. Then everything was swallowed in a red gush of blood. I immediately wrapped my right hand in a fist around both fingers to apply pressure and held both hands above my head, and clearly remember saying to Will, "I just lost one, maybe two fingers. We need to get to a hospital now!"

The area had no cell signal, I didn't own a satellite communicator at the time, and we hadn't passed anyone all day. Given that the sun was setting and I could still walk, self-rescue seemed like the right call. I dropped my crash pads, had Will grab a small pack containing my wallet, keys, and headlamp, and we set off down the creek. With my hand still clutched above my head, I kept a steady but brisk pace, consciously trying not to spike my heart rate and increase the bleeding. Many downed trees presented tricky obstacles to clear without the use of my hands. After about half an hour, we made it back to the car.

It took us another 15 minutes of driving before we had cell signal, at which point I decided an ambulance would be slower (and more expensive), so we just continued on our own. It took us about an hour more to reach the emergency room in Monroe. A couple of hours later, I was transferred to a hospital in Kirkland, where I underwent surgery around midnight.

Whether exploring boulderfields or attempting high peaks, many climbers are injured by loose rock during their approaches and descents. (A) Here, a climber's fingers were crushed against the slab at left when his foothold and handhold broke free. (B) The large block that pulled loose. *Jamie Sookprasong*

ANALYSIS

Given that we descended the same path and everything had felt secure on the way up, my hypothesis is that warming temperatures during the day may have thawed some ice or frozen soil holding the blocks in place. Will's lighter weight likely wasn't enough to break the foothold, or perhaps he descended slightly differently.

I now always carry a satellite communicator, so I can get help in areas without a cell signal. We also should have carried a real first-aid kit—we essentially just had a pair of gloves and some band-aids. (*Source: Jamie Sookprasong.*)

VARIOUS RESCUES | Climber Falls and Rockfall
Cascade Range, Mt. Stuart

On July 29, a 23-year-old woman was struck by rockfall near the top of the north ridge of Mt. Stuart and took a long fall as a result. She was seriously injured, with a head injury and fractured arm and leg. A Naval air rescue team tried to reach the climber twice, later the same night and then again in the morning, but the combination of altitude, wind, and hot weather limited the helicopter's capability.

Instead, a team from Chelan County Mountain Rescue was flown in by Chelan County helicopters and then ascended to the climber's position. Through the afternoon and evening, the rescuers lowered her about 1,000 feet down the northwest face of the mountain to reach the Stuart Glacier, where additional team members met them. A Navy helicopter was able to evacuate her at about 11:30 p.m. on July 30, more than 24 hours after the accident. She was reported to be in satisfactory condition at the hospital.

On the other side of the mountain, two climbers were rescued after falls in the Cascadian Couloir, in May and July. Both suffered broken legs and required helicopter evacuation.

ANALYSIS

Regarding the late-July incident on Stuart's north ridge, posts at Chelan County Mountain Rescue's Facebook page said, "Yesterday's rescue mission on the NW Face of Mt. Stuart was a model of cooperative task management in the face of great challenges and while confronting immense danger.... Thanks sincerely to Craig Gyselinck [Field Team Leader], Jacob Leonard, Nathan Richmond, Vern Nelson, Jonah Manning, and Jason Schilling for accomplishing one of the most complex, dangerous and difficult rescues ever done on Mt. Stuart." (*Source: News reports, Chelan County Mountain Rescue.*)

After helicopters could not reach an injured climber near the top of Mt. Stuart, rescuers climbed to her and then lowered her about 1,000 feet down the steep northwest face to the Stuart Glacier, where a helicopter could evacuate her. *Chelan County Mountain Rescue*

SKIING FALL
Mt. Rainier, Liberty Ridge

In the afternoon of June 26, Matthew Bunker (28) was descending on skis when he fell on steep terrain around 10,400 feet, just below Thumb Rock, the high camp for the Liberty Ridge route. His partner reported Bunker missing at about 3 p.m. Climbing rangers conducted several aerial searches, but severe winds and clouds hampered search efforts until June 29, when a ranger spotted Bunker's body in a crevasse. Park officials said they were unable to recover the body because of continuous rockfall and icefall hazards. (*Source: Mt. Rainier National Park.*)

ANALYSIS

It's unknown what caused the skier to fall. Depending on the snow surface, it would have been difficult to impossible for a skier to arrest a slide on this terrain. (*Source: The Editors.*)

WEST VIRGINIA

GROUND FALL | Cam Pulled Out
Cooper's Rock State Forest, Roof Rocks

On October 4, I (Mike Paugh, 38) and Sarah Smith were searching for areas at Cooper's Rock to bring clients with my new guide service, Ascension Climbing Guides. We were also climbing routes in the area. At about 2 p.m., I racked up to attempt Upchouca (5.12a/b), which begins with an unprotected V5 start. I knew the route was in my wheelhouse of climbing fitness but also at the peak of my climbing limits. I felt confident about the send. I rehearsed the opening moves 10 to 12 times, trying to find my sequence to the hero jug about 15 feet up.

I set off one last time, committing to the boulder problem and fully aware there was a point of no return where I could not jump off without getting injured. I felt gassed and pumped immediately after making it through the crux, probably from the numerous attempts to figure out my sequence. Unfortunately, the placement I had spotted from the ground for my first piece of protection turned out to be complete garbage.

Feeling pumped and realizing that I was in trouble, I continued upward and found an excellent horizontal seam. I placed a yellow Metolius TCU up to the

Mike Paugh had set up a video camera to record what he hoped would be an onsight of a 5.12 route at Cooper's Rock. The site of the cam that pulled out is marked. *Video capture courtesy of Mike Paugh*

trigger, with all three lobes fully engaged, and clipped it using an alpine draw. Breathing a sigh of relief, I asked my belayer, Sarah, to take me. The cam held and I proceeded to shake out my arms. The climbing above looked to ease up significantly, and I identified a couple of solid gear placements.

As soon as I shifted my body weight to the left and prepared to continue up the route, the TCU blew from the rock with the sound of a 12-gauge shotgun. When it popped, a piece of rock hit me in the face as I began to fall. Everything sped up, and the next thing I remember is hitting the ground and screaming in pain. I suffered an open fracture of my left tibia and fibula. Thankfully, there was a party of four climbers nearby who responded to Sarah's call for help until EMS arrived.

ANALYSIS

I had three surgeries to repair the damage and later remove the external fixation device attached to my leg. I've been doing great with my recovery, and I've started climbing again.

Given the hard, bouldery crux in the first 15 to 18 feet of this route and the rocky landing below it, I should have placed bouldering pads at the base of the climb, treating it like a highball boulder problem. Protecting the landing zone should have been priority number one, especially for a ground-up, on-sight attempt. Once I reached the jug hold past the crux, I was in a no-return, no-fall zone, especially without any pad protection.

I've also realized I should have considered setting up a top-rope to rehearse the route, due to its PG-13 rating and not being able to assess gear placements adequately from the ground. Had I done so, I could have safely assessed the rock quality (which was a little chossy in the crack) and the protection before leading. I also could have backed up that single TCU with another placement before asking Sarah to take my weight.

I am extremely grateful to the group of young climbers who kept me calm and called 911 and to everyone who helped get me out of there and care for my injuries. (*Source: Mike Paugh.*)

FALL ON ROCK | Broken Hold
New River Gorge, Endless Wall, Party Buttress

It was November 21, and our day started by warming up on Riding the Crest of the Wave (5.9 trad) at Idol Point. We then walked to Party Buttress to attempt Harbinger Scarab (5.12c), a 100-foot, mostly bolted route that requires a couple of traditional pieces down low. Markus Kauffman (23) climbed through the roof crux, which is four or five bolts up, and was making his way up the steep headwall above. He was past the seventh bolt and about 30 feet past the roof when the accident occurred.

Markus had rested at the seventh bolt so he could work out the sequence above. He then made a couple more moves and began a final dynamic move off his right hand. At that point, I heard him scream, "Rock!" and saw Markus falling along with a softball-size piece of rock—the right handhold had broken. The rock did not strike him as he fell. There was an appropriate amount of slack in the system, and I gave him a dynamic catch as I have hundreds of other times. But what should have been a benign fall, if his body remained upright, turned into one that involved a rescue and me writing an accident report.

Pulling hard with his right hand and ripping off the hold must have thrown Markus off-balance and created enough momentum to cause him to invert and twist, so the right side of his head struck the wall. I called up to him to see if he was okay. He did not respond, and his body was limp. I lowered him to the ground and began to assess the situation. I called for help, did a primary trauma assessment, and made sure Markus did not move his neck. Another climber called 911 at 11:15 a.m.

Markus regained consciousness within one minute of being lowered to the ground and knew his name and where he was after a few minutes. A group of climbers helped me care for him while we waited for help. The Fayette County High Angle Rescue

Team arrived at 1:45 p.m. via fixed lines above the nearby climb, Smooth Operator (5.9). Markus was in a helicopter around 2:40 p.m. and flown to a nearby hospital. He suffered multiple fractures on the right side of his face, multiple lacerations on his face and forehead, and was diagnosed with a small subdural hematoma in his frontal lobe at the hospital. He was discharged after three days in the hospital.

ANALYSIS

Markus was not wearing a helmet. Wearing one, even while sport climbing, can decrease the risk of injury during rockfall and in the event of bad lead fall, or at least lessen the severity of the injury. Knocking on holds and not using ones that sound hollow is a good habit. Lastly, carry a good first-aid kit and exchange the phone numbers of emergency contacts with climbing partners. (*Source: Nick Rico.*)

WISCONSIN

TOP-ROPE ANCHOR FAILURE | Sling Cut by Sharp Rock
Devil's Lake, Gill's Buttress

In the afternoon of June 21, a party of four was top-roping Gill's Nose, a 5.11 route at Gill's Buttress. The top-rope had been set up by Person 2. Three of the climbers had climbed on the route, falling and lowering safely without any issues. Climber 1 was the last on the route and was tasked with cleaning. He did not fall until the upper section's crux. He describes feeling the rope catch him, but a moment later he started free falling. The rope and the carabiners at the masterpoint fell with the climber. He hit a slab toward the bottom of the climb and came to rest within 15 feet of the base. In total he fell approximately 50 feet.

This sling was tied to create a masterpoint loop for a top-rope anchor. The loop apparently rubbed against a sharp edge and cut.

The climber sustained two collapsed lungs, six broken ribs, a broken scapula, a broken leg, a puncture in his right shin, a burn across his neck, a punctured bladder, and abrasions across his body. An EMT and WFA were on the scene immediately and placed the climber into recovery position on his left side after noting the most extensive damage was right-sided. Within 10 minutes, park staff were organizing the rescue. It took approximately an hour to litter and move the patient to a safe zone for a helicopter. He was then airlifted out of the park to receive emergency care. The patient was expected to make a full recovery.

ANALYSIS

The top-rope anchor was set up in two parts. First, a large boulder on top of Gill's Buttress was slung as protection. To extend the anchor closer to the edge, a 60m

Black Diamond nylon runner (about two years old and used only three times as intended) was clipped to the protection with a figure-8 knot. This sling was tied into a masterpoint with a second figure-8 knot. Two locking carabiners were attached to the masterpoint, and the rope was threaded through these carabiners. The accident occurred due to a failure of the nylon runner in the masterpoint loop, causing the rope, carabiners, and Climber 1 to fall to the ground, while the rest of the anchor remained on top.

The protection used, a large boulder, was an excellent choice for the area. However, the extension could have been improved by using thick, abrasion-resistant static rope. Otherwise, cordelette (long enough to be doubled) or two separate slings should have been used. Two loops in the masterpoint might have prevented this accident.

Pictures of the sling indicate a relatively clean, linear cut. The quartzite at Devil's Lake is known for sharp edges, and climbers must be diligent in inspecting the rock at edges, corners, and breaks, including areas the anchor materials could "walk" to. It is unknown if the masterpoint had significant travel. Most likely, the direction of pull during Climber 1's fall partially cut the sling, and a moment after he weighted the rope, the nylon separated at the weakness. (*Source: Close associate of Climber 1.*)

EDITOR'S NOTE: *In addition to creating a redundant top-rope anchor, consider padding the rock beneath anchor materials to protect against abrasion or cuts.*

WYOMING

FALL ON SNOW
Grand Teton National Park, South Teton, Cave Couloir

On July 4, a party of two male climbers climbed the South Teton from their camp in the Meadows of Garnet Canyon. They were using ice axes and crampons and wearing helmets. During the late afternoon and early evening, several thunderstorms passed over the Tetons. As the party dealt with these storms, they realized they were descending a slope they had not traveled during their ascent earlier in the day. At approximately 8 p.m., one of the climbers (age 32) slipped and fell near the top of the Cave Couloir, which rises above Garnet Meadows. [*Another person who observed these climbers believes the man attempted to glissade and lost control.*] He slid approximately 200 feet on snow, stopping after impacting a large boulder. He sustained serious injuries to the left side of his body, including a suspected broken femur or femoral head.

The partner descended to the Meadows, where he contacted a person with a cell phone. At approximately 9:20 p.m., the call was forwarded to the on-duty SAR coordinator, and the caller relayed the location of the incident and provided GPS coordinates. She also mentioned that the partner had grabbed a sleeping bag and was climbing back up to the injured climber.

Climbing rangers Ronczkowski and Hunsaker departed the Lupine Meadows trailhead at 10:30 p.m. They reached the injured climber at 12:55 a.m., assessed and stabilized his injuries, and made him as comfortable as possible for the night. At 6 a.m., the SAR coordinator talked with the rangers on scene via radio and decided a short-haul extraction was needed. Several hours later, the climber was flown to Lupine Meadows, arriving at 9:25 a.m., and transferred to an ambulance. (*Source: Grand Teton National Park Search and Rescue Report.*)

ANALYSIS

Although many factors likely contributed to this accident, the late hour, storms, and fatigue undoubtedly played key roles. These climbers would have been much better off if they had turned back before the summit instead of pushing on and experiencing storms that delayed and tired them, increasing the likelihood they would stray from the correct descent and, possibly, make the decision to glissade an unknown slope. (*Source: The Editors.*)

CREVASSE FALL | Hypothermia
Grand Teton National Park, Teton Glacier

After descending from Mt. Owen via rappels in the Koven Couloir, a two-person climbing party (Kia M., Ryan S.) came upon a distressed climber (Josh A.) in the flats of Teton Glacier at about 9:20 p.m. on August 8. Josh explained that his partner, Tyler, age 34, had disappeared into a crevasse about 20 minutes prior to their arrival. Tyler had fallen roughly 25 feet into the crevasse, which was estimated to be 45 feet deep. He was stuck sideways in a horizontal position in a constriction in the crevasse. Josh had prepared the lip of the crevasse and lowered a rope to Tyler, but Tyler was unable to secure himself nor manage prusiks to ascend out of the crevasse.

Tyler had been unroped but was wearing a helmet and a harness. He was in shorts, a cotton shirt, and light insulating jacket. He was not wearing crampons and had limited mobility of his arms and hands. His backpack was partially attached to him. The crevasse hole at the surface was roughly five feet by four feet.

An SOS text message was attempted at roughly 10 p.m. via a Garmin inReach, but limited view of the sky prevented its successful sending.

Two deadman snow anchors were constructed uphill of the crevasse in heavy, wet snow. A 3:1 Z-drop haul system was assembled, using prusiks and a Tibloc traction device. A large bowline was lowered to Tyler in an attempt to raise him by his armpits, since access to his harness was prevented by his position in the crevasse.

With two people hauling on the Z-drop and the third tending the progress prusik, Tyler was raised roughly 20 feet. The original lip, prepared by Tyler's partner, had morphed into a ceiling in the remaining snow bridge, preventing Tyler from making a smooth exit onto the surface. Feeling extreme pain from the pressure of the rope and worried he would fall, Tyler urgently asked to be lowered. He ended up back in his original position, 25 feet down and stuck in the constriction, with no access to his harness.

A new lip in the crevasse was prepared and Ryan, using a long loop on the unused length of the 60-meter rope, rappelled into the crevasse to reach Tyler, who was now minimally vocal and responsive. He was covered in snow and completely wet. Ryan was able to secure the rope to Tyler's belay loop with a locking carabiner and then

climbed back out of the crevasse. Tyler complained that he could not use his hands and that his arms felt broken.

At 10:20 p.m., the climbers again attempted to raise Tyler. However, his wedged position prevented upward progress. A 5:1 Z-drop system was rigged for more power, but abandoned due to friction in the wet rope and small diameter carabiners. Josh was then lowered into the crevasse via a top belay in an attempt to unstick Tyler from his position. Tyler was freed and raised to the new crevasse lip at roughly 10:45 p.m. He was intermittently moaning and nearly completely unresponsive; he had contusions on his left eye and exposed knees. With Josh slightly below Tyler in the crevasse, the climbers were able to rig a shoulder harness onto Tyler and secure it to the haul line, in order to pull him over the lip.

Tyler was removed from the crevasse at roughly 11:10 p.m. He had been in the crevasse nearly two hours. His wet upper clothes were removed and replaced with a light jacket, along with head coverings.

Weighing the competing risks of exposure versus exacerbating any potential spinal or head injuries, and because Tyler previously had not complained of major injury, the team elected to move Tyler off the snow and exposure to wind on the glacier.

(Top) Rangers tend to hypothermic climber awaiting helicopter rescue. Approximate crevasse location is circled. (Bottom) The accident scene below Mt. Owen. (A) Koven Couloir. (B) Crevasse. (C) Bivy site. *Ryan Stolp*

Unsure if there were other crevasses in the area, the party roped up in a glacier configuration and attempted to create a litter to tow Tyler to dry land, roughly 70 yards to the north. Unable to securely move him this way, the party resorted to incremental lifts, supporting his head.

At 11:45, Tyler was situated at the edge of the glacier on the first dirt and rock available. A platform of rocks, ropes, and backpacks was created in an attempt to insulate him. He was completely unresponsive at this time, infrequently moaning and snoring. He had foam at the mouth and intermittent spasms of his legs and arms, which demanded constant tending to keep him covered in his makeshift clothing.

A successful inReach message was sent and acknowledged by Grand Teton National Park at 11:45 p.m., but continued poor reception prevented the climbers from replying. Rangers Shain and Evans began hiking to the Teton Glacier at approximately 12:30 a.m. Tyler's partner snuggled up to him to provide body warmth, and the climbers monitored his vitals. The two climbing rangers located the climbers a little after 4 a.m. With new and dry supplies, Tyler was layered and wrapped, and a platform for a short-haul litter was created. A ranger actively warmed Tyler with his body heat and hands. By 7 a.m., Tyler was verbal and aware of his surroundings. He had memory of his fall and the incident.

Arrangements were made to fly Tyler directly to Eastern Idaho Regional Medical Center. Soon, rangers arrived by helicopter and dropped off a litter and full-body vacuum mattress, as a precaution because of spinal injuries. A little after 8 a.m., Tyler was short-hauled off the glacier to Lupine Meadows, where he was transferred to an air ambulance. The rest of the party followed in two subsequent flights to Lupine Meadows. Tyler was treated for hypothermia and discharged after a few days, with some lingering nerve damage in his hands.

ANALYSIS

There is no record of any prior crevasse fall on the lower Teton Glacier in this publication's archives. This crevasse was in a nearly flat section near the toe of the glacier. The many climbers who cross this part of the glacier while hiking to or from Mt. Owen rarely if ever rope up. One reasonable precaution before crossing any snowfield or glacier is to cover all skin (long pants vs. shorts) as protection against abrasion in a fall; however, additional clothes were unlikely to prevent Tyler's hypothermia after being inside a wet crevasse for two hours.

The two climbers who came upon this scene after a long day in the mountains, along with Tyler's partner, worked through the night to save him—a highly commendable effort. (*Sources: Ryan Stolp, Grand Teton National Park Search and Rescue Report, Sharp End Podcast episode 58 interview with Tyler Willis.*)

FALL NEAR SUMMIT
Grand Teton National Park, Grand Teton, Exum Ridge

At approximately 6:45 p.m. on September 10, the SAR coordinator on duty was connected with a caller who said he and his partner were at the "Boulder Problem in the Sky," near the top of the Exum Ridge and the summit of the Grand Teton. The partner, age 45, had injured her right knee during a short ground-level slip and could not descend the mountain. The injured woman and her partner had departed from Lupine Meadows trailhead at 3 a.m. for a planned one-day ascent via the Upper Exum Ridge route.

With nightfall not far away, Helicopter 35HX was immediately requested and arrived at Lupine Meadows at 7 p.m. After a reconnaissance of the summit area, the helicopter and crew landed at the Lower Saddle to rig for short haul. Ranger Bellino was inserted to the Boulder Problem in the Sky at 7:33 p.m., and he put the patient in a screamer suit for extraction. Bellino and the injured climber were lifted from the site and flown to Lupine Meadows by 7:45 p.m. The partner descended on his own.

ANALYSIS

Rangers see lots of seemingly small slips that become fairly big issues in places like approaches to crags or talus fields. In this case, it was at the summit of Wyoming's second-highest peak and it necessitated a helicopter rescue. Fatigue may have contributed to this accident. A one-day ascent of the Grand Teton from the road is a feat that should be attempted by experienced climbers in top physical condition. (*Sources: Grand Teton National Park Search and Rescue Report and the Editors.*)

ROCKFALL CAUSES ANCHOR FAILURE
Wind River Range, Pingora Peak

Four climbers summited Pingora Peak in the Cirque of the Towers on September 5 and started down the south buttress. They chose to rappel a line to the left of the main south buttress route, using two ropes tied together. Two of them had used this descent two days earlier.

They team completed the first rappel and gathered at the next anchor, consisting of slings around a boulder. As one of the climbers pulled the ropes from their first rappel, a rock came down the face and smashed into the anchor, cutting both slings around the boulder. Janette Heung, 35, had been clipped into the anchor, and she fell when it was cut. One of the other climbers also began to fall, but was able to grab a sling girth-hitched to the harness of one of his companions. The climbers, none of whom were now connected to any anchor, quickly secured themselves and each other to an older adjacent anchor. Heung fell about 400 feet to the ground.

One of the climbers used an inReach to contact search and rescue. The team built a new anchor and descended to Heung's location. They attempted to revive her but were unsuccessful. A helicopter with a crew from Tip Top Search and Rescue arrived about one hour after the fall and continued resuscitation efforts, but Heung succumbed to her injuries.

ANALYSIS

Janette Heung was an expert alpine and ice climber, and her partners are highly experienced as well. The climbers believe that pulling the rappel rope dislodged the rock that fell. The anchor materials at their stance consisted of a recently placed double-length Dyneema sling and an older, UV-damaged loop of tubular webbing, connected by a quick-link.

This was a tragic and unusual accident, and it's not certain that anything specific could have been done to prevent it. As general advice for such rappels, take care to position the rappel ropes to avoid potentially loose horns, flakes, or rocks on ledges, and consider backing up fixed rappel anchors during transitions from one rappel to the next. It costs little time to plug a cam into a crack and clip into it directly—this is especially important for larger groups and/or crowded stances. (*Sources: Climbing partner's report on Mountain Project, Rock and Ice magazine, and the Editors.*)

FALL FROM BASE OF ROUTE
Wind River Range, War Bonnet Peak

On August 2, Junghyun "Jiji" Nam fell at the base of the Feather Buttress route (5.10+) on the north side of War Bonnet Peak, above the Cirque of the Towers. Nam and her climbing partner were gearing up to start the climb when she slipped and tumbled an estimated 80 to 100 feet down the steep approach route. She was helicoptered from the scene with serious injuries and several days later was removed from life support at the hospital.

ANALYSIS
The approaches to many climbs involve scrambling to a high belay ledge before the roped climbing begins. Careful movement is essential while preparing to tie in and anchor for the first pitch. In some cases, it may be prudent to put on harnesses and other gear before the final approach, to avoid these maneuvers on a small, exposed stance. It's also a good idea to don one's helmet before the final approach to alpine routes. (*Source: The Editors.*)

LEADER FALL ON ICE | Inadequate Protection
Cody, South Fork Valley

On February 8, I took a long leader fall on the third pitch of Broken Hearts, a long ice route in the South Fork Valley. I was climbing in a group of three ahead of five friends doing the same route in two rope teams. At around 11 a.m., I was near the top of the WI3+ pitch when I made a poor placement with one tool. As I was removing my other tool for the next placement, the first tool popped and I fell.

I was climbing with 8.2mm half ropes and clipping every other screw with them. My last screw was approximately six feet below my boots when I fell. I impacted a slanting shelf about 20 feet down, hitting my pelvis and back, and then continued to fall another 10 feet or so. My partner was able to get me to the snow ledge below, and we called for help.

Various climbers in the area as well as members of Park County Search and Rescue, Cody Regional Wilderness Medical Team, and Big Horn County Search and Rescue responded. Rescuers reached the scene at about 2:30 p.m. I was put in a litter and lowered two pitches to the ground, then carried to a tracked snow vehicle, which took me to an ambulance. My pelvis was fractured in three places, and I had a fractured sacrum, a compression fracture in the L1 vertebra, and a broken rib. (*Sources: Rick Dvorak, 42, and Park County Sheriff's Office.*)

ANALYSIS
Given the length of many ice pitches, the thin ropes often used, and the fact that belayers are often positioned some distance from the base of the climb (adding slack to the system), any ice climbing leader fall is likely to be quite long. To minimize the risk of serious injury, climbers should place frequent protection and, above all, take care to ensure that every tool and crampon placement is solid before moving to the next. (*Source: The Editors.*)

Rescuers at the site of a fall into a moat (marked) on Chimai Mountain. The party had been descending steep snow behind the rock arête, left of the rescuers, when one slipped. *Squamish Search and Rescue*

CANADA

FALL INTO MOAT | Climbing Unroped, Exposure
British Columbia, Coast Mountains, Chimai Mountain

Seven mountaineering club members had planned a climb of Chimai Mountain (2,306 meters), northwest of Squamish, in July. Although the mountain is glaciated, online research had suggested there was a route to the top that did not involve glacier travel. As a result, they took no ropes but did carry ice axes, crampons, and helmets.

On July 18, they made an early start from a logging road at the bottom of the valley. During the ascent, two members of the group fell behind while the remaining climbers continued on to reach the summit by midafternoon. The final leg of the ascent involved a short diagonal route along a narrow snow line between a small bergschrund feature and a large moat just below. While descending the same route, one member of the group (male, mid-50s) slipped in the soft snow above the moat and, unable to stop, slid over the edge and free-fell about four meters before entering the moat, striking rock outcrops along the way. The individual landed on rock approximately five meters below the lip of the moat.

The party activated a satellite distress beacon while attempting to provide aid to the injured person, who was responsive. Without a rope, they were unable to extricate the stranded member, though they were able to get extra clothing to him.

Due to the remote location, it was well over an hour before Squamish Search and Rescue was able to reach the site via helicopter. Rescuers found the subject standing in the bottom of the moat but, due to language difficulties, were not able to communicate with him. After building snow anchors, a rescuer rappelled into the moat and attached a rescue harness to the patient, so he and the rescuer could be raised out of the moat. At the hospital, the patient was found to have serious head trauma and a spinal injury.

All of the other party members were mildly hypothermic, as they had given all of their extra clothing to the patient. The entire team, including the two members who had stopped well below the summit, was flown out by helicopter.

ANALYSIS

When traveling on soft snow, especially on a western aspect in the afternoon, crampon spikes may not penetrate sufficiently through the snow layer to provide secure footing. Also, crampons may ball up with wet snow. Careful plunge-stepping and use of an ice axe are required to remain secure.

An awareness of hazards below might have helped the party pick a better descent route. While avoiding crevasses, the climbing party exposed themselves to other hazards, and without a rope they did not have the ability to protect themselves or perform a companion rescue. It should be noted that moats can be deeper than crevasses, and they also can hold numerous rock outcroppings—as in this case—so a fall can easily result in serious injury.

Mountaineers should be prepared to undertake a rescue because an organized rescue may be some time away, even in good weather. They also should take extra clothing and gear to deal with an emergency. In this case, the party members had only a single extra layer each, which they gave to the injured party, leaving themselves exposed to the cold. This turned the entire party into rescue subjects. Members of this group also became separated, reducing the number of people available to provide assistance and prolonging the rescue. (*Source: Bob Manson, Squamish Search and Rescue.*)

FATAL FALL | Climbing Unroped
British Columbia, Glacier National Park, Mt. Sir Donald

On August 16, an experienced climber fell 250 meters to his death while moving unroped on the northwest ridge of Mt. Sir Donald. Reports suggested the 25-year-old man fell after pulling off a large block or boulder. Parks Canada was notified about the accident at around 8 a.m., and the fallen climber was located during a helicopter search.

ANALYSIS

The northwest ridge of Mt. Sir Donald is rated 5.4, with substantial sections of fourth-class climbing. Because of the climb's length (approximately 2,400 vertical feet), it is common to ascend and descend large portions of the route unroped. The quartzite of Mt. Sir Donald is notoriously slippery when wet, but the weather was hot and dry on the day of the accident. (*Source: News reports.*)

FATAL FALLS | Inexperience, Off Route on Descent
Alberta, Jasper National Park, Mt. Edith Cavell

A 32-year-old male and a 25-year-old female attempted Mt. Edith Cavell via the third-class west ridge during the weekend of September 19 and 20. It is not known if they reached the summit, but there is evidence they got high on the ridge. During their descent, in darkness and poor weather, they apparently got off route while trying to find their way down into the West Bowl and they entered fifth-class terrain. Without a rope, one of the party members fell, and it is believed the second member fell while attempting to go for help. Their bodies were discovered during a helicopter search at 6 p.m. on September 20.

ANALYSIS

The party had less than one year of experience. They had inadequate clothing and equipment for this route, including running shoes that would have been slippery while downclimbing wet quartzite rock; the poor weather may have caused exposure and contributed to poor decision making. They had not informed anyone about the details of their outing, delaying a search. (*Source: Jasper National Park.*)

Climbers wait for help near the east ridge of Mt. Temple. *Parks Canada*

LEADER FALL | Off Route, Loose Rock
Alberta, Banff National Park, Mt. Temple

September 12 started out on the wrong foot for a pair of experienced climbers and outdoor recreationalists. They had not climbed on this part of Mt. Temple and were "off route" nearly as soon as they shut the car door at 3 a.m.

Unfamiliar with the area, the two individuals hiked up the wrong access gully for their intended route on the east ridge of Mt. Temple (IV 5.7). Traveling by headlamp, the climbers associated certain terrain features with the route description and were baffled by others. Just above treeline, where the rock rises dramatically upward, fewer options become available. Still believing they were on the right route, the lead climber left the comfort of a good belay ledge and ascended a blocky corner system. At this point, they were roughly 100 meters to climber's left of the actual line, venturing into terrain that likely had not been touched by human hands.

The leader had made some vertical progress before grabbing a block approximately one cubic foot in size with the right hand. The leader fully weighted the block, which gave way, spinning off its perch and crashing into the trees beneath them. As the rock dislodged, the lead climber fell back, spinning 360 degrees and making first contact with the rock with the right foot. The leader tumbled over the rocky ledges for several more meters, coming to rest on a small ledge below the belayer and just above a large cliff. The climber sustained a broken right ankle and various cuts and bruises.

The two climbers triggered the SOS on an inReach device and were able to contact Banff Dispatch to initiate a rescue. Both climbers were trained in first aid and were able to bandage and splint the injured ankle appropriately before the rescue team arrived.

ANALYSIS

The rescued party was well prepared with regard to first aid, communication, and overall mountain skill. However, the two climbers could have researched their route more thoroughly and scoped out the line in daylight to find the correct ridge-line feature. Once on the mountain, they could have taken more time to figure out where they were, using the route description, GPS, Google Earth, or similar resources. (They had cell service.) A little more time spent on research and planning may have prevented this accident. (*Source: Banff, Yoho & Kootenay National Parks Visitor Safety Team.*)

STRANDED | Dropped Crampon, Weather and Darkness
Alberta, Banff National Park, Mt. Temple

On August 1, a party of two was ascending the east ridge of Mt. Temple and navigating a section of the route that involved traversing steep ice and snow for several hundred meters before the final vertical step through a rock band called the Black Towers. While on this section of the route, one of the party members dropped a crampon down the steep southeast face and was unable to retrieve it. The party attempted to descend the east ridge but got caught in a thunderstorm with heavy rainfall soon after they started down.

With diminishing daylight and the route completely wet, the climbers called for help at 10 p.m. Rescue personnel advised the group to find a sheltered place to spend the night. A successful long-line rescue was initiated at dawn the next day.

ANALYSIS
The party was able to effectively retreat to terrain that was suitable for an emergency bivy. They also used good judgment to not continue their descent after the thunderstorm. The steep quartzite rock bands on the east ridge get extremely slick and treacherous when wet. As well, the climbing party was carrying an appropriate communication device to initiate a rescue.

Inspect all your equipment to ensure that it is in good working order before every outing. When switching to terrain that will require different equipment, such as moving from vertical rock to snow and ice, it is best to find or make a platform that allows for a comfortable transition. This will reduce the risk of dropping gear and allow for a more effective check to ensure the equipment has been adjusted correctly. (*Source: Banff, Yoho & Kootenay National Parks Visitor Safety Team.*)

STEEP SKIING FALL | Variable Snow Conditions
Alberta, Banff National Park, Mt. Temple

Our party of three arrived at the Moraine Lake parking lot around 7:30 a.m. on December 28. The focus of the day was to ski the Pinnacle-Eiffel Couloir in Paradise Valley. We expected to cover the roughly 12-kilometer approach in three to four hours. Temperatures were reasonable (-10°C to -8°C), with no precipitation expected, and the light was good. We felt there were no issues from an avalanche or weather perspective.

We found an old skin track once we reached Paradise Creek, which we followed to the base of the north face of Mt. Temple (about two hours from the car). We were making decent time, but we could tell the conditions would not be ideal for skiing the Eiffel line, so we decided we would try to return later in the week for that, and

Overview of the Cobra Couloir and the skiers' position after a long fall. The party dug a platform in the middle of the couloir for helicopter access and moved the injured skier from the original location by the steep right wall. *Parks Canada*

we would head to the Cobra Couloir on Mt. Temple instead.

As we approached the line, the snow was pretty much bulletproof. We transferred to boot-packing fairly low because skins were inefficient without ski crampons, due to the hard snow surface. As we boot-packed up the line, we discussed the variability in the snow. Depending on which runnel we chose to follow, it varied from almost ice to knee-deep soft snow. We knew the skiing would not be great, but we decided to push on.

We reached the top of the couloir roughly 1.5 hours later and transitioned to ski. As two skiers watched from above, the first skier started down, and it was obvious the snow was variable. We had discussed regrouping at a certain feature in the line, but the skier decided to continue past that point. As the skier crossed the slope to make a turn, they were pushed slightly uphill and thrown toward the tails of their skis. The momentum could not be stopped, and they slid backward down the couloir. We lost sight of the falling skier as they went around a small corner. We heard a loud bang seconds later and then heard nothing.

We waited approximately 10 to 15 seconds and then started to descend, moving very cautiously. We came across one pole, then another, and a ski, at which point we were able to see the skier, roughly 300 vertical meters below us on the slope, and make vocal contact.

The skier's face showed some blood from a split lip, and they expressed concerns about knee and shoulder injuries. An initial assessment for head trauma was made, and the helmet was checked for signs of impact. Both were negative. The fallen skier was wrapped with additional warm layers and stabilized in position. We then sent an SOS on our inReach device. We knew a helicopter would not be able to maneuver into the space where we were located, as we were fairly close to the wall of the couloir, so we decided to move the skier to the middle of the couloir after a platform was cleared. There, we continued to treat the skier with hot liquid, energy gels, and a couple of painkillers. The helicopter crew was able to fly into the area and remove the skier via long-line rescue. From the SOS signal to the extraction of the skier, the time was roughly one hour and 40 minutes.

With enough daylight remaining, the two others skied back to the car. The injured skier was later released from the hospital with a reset shoulder and a knee injury that was expected to heal with physical therapy. This was a lucky outcome, considering the potential injuries from a fall in this location. (*Source: Member of the ski party.*)

ANALYSIS

Inherent in skiing a steep, big mountain couloir is the risk of falling and not being able to stop. There are several things people can do to mitigate this risk. First, wait for optimal surface conditions (i.e., softer snow or consistent snow). Often it is tricky to balance avalanche risk with the risk of falling. Second, ensure that all party members are expert skiers. Further, ensure the equipment is appropriate and will function properly (appropriately adjusted ski bindings, boots and skis free of ice buildup, helmets secured). At a certain level, all party members must be willing to accept that it will be very difficult or impossible to arrest a fall. Usually, when people fall in a steep couloir like this, they end up at the bottom on flatter terrain. Stopping partway down likely contributed to the injured skier's positive outcome.

From the rescuer's perspective, the party did a good job of moving the injured skier to a location that was accessible with a helicopter long line. They also did well to shovel a large, flat landing area for the rescuer to detach from the long line and package the patient. One thing to consider when choosing a spot for a helicopter pickup is any overhead hazard. In this case, it was a cool day with minimal winds, so nothing was moving in the couloir. However, when possible—and when it allows enough clearance for a helicopter to fly overhead—it is better to be situated where there is more shelter from snow or rocks that may fall down the couloir. (*Source: Banff, Yoho & Kootenay National Parks Visitor Safety Team.*)

FALL ON ROCK | Wall Impact
Alberta, Banff National Park, Lake Louise

On July 22, three climbers were on The Search, a 5.10 sport route at the Back of the Lake crag. This pitch starts off a large ledge about 20 meters above the ground. At around 3 p.m., the leader fell while climbing above the fourth bolt and impacted the cliff with one leg. It was a strange, twisting fall that resulted in an injury to the left knee (shattered patella). The leader was lowered back to the ledge by the belayer, and they called Banff Dispatch for help. The injured climber was in too much pain to be lowered to the ground by the two partners.

The Banff Visitor Safety team responded with a helicopter from Canmore. The team initially thought they might be able to heli-sling onto the ledge. However, after a test run without rescuers on the line, it was decided the terrain above was too overhanging for that technique. The rescuers landed nearby and walked and climbed to access the ledge. After splinting the injury and administering some pain medication, they lowered the climber to the ground in a stretcher.

ANALYSIS

The Search is gently overhanging and has a cruxy start. It is common for people to fall at the first or second bolt, where they risk a ledge fall. In this accident, the climber fell at the fourth bolt and impacted the cliff in a sideways fashion, injuring one knee. The reason given for the fall was sweaty hands. It was a warm day for the area, about 25°C.

Falling safely while rock climbing is a learned skill, as is belaying sport climbs, where falls are to be expected. Sometimes a tight belay (a "hard catch") will cause the climber to swing into the wall with greater force, but it is not certain this was a contributing factor. While belaying a leader on a climb like The Search, the belayer needs to weigh the risk of giving the climber a softer catch and longer fall (and potentially a ledge fall) versus a shorter fall and potentially harder catch. This situation is fairly common in sport climbing, and the leader and belayer should discuss the risks and appropriate belay before each new climb. (*Source: Banff, Yoho & Kootenay National Parks Visitor Safety Team.*)

FALL WHILE ATTEMPTING NEW ROUTE | Loose Rock
Alberta, Banff National Park, Saddleback Wall

On July 28, two climbers were attempting a new route on the quartzite cliff known as the Saddleback Wall, near Lake Louise. They were one or two pitches up the four-pitch wall when the leader pulled off a loose block and took a fall. The gear held, but the falling leader swung hard into the wall and injured one ankle. The climbers were able to rappel to the ground and started to walk out, but then realized the walk would be very slow and painful, so they called for a rescue.

ANALYSIS
The Canadian Rockies have a wide range of rock types and quality. Although the quartzite cliffs of the Saddleback Wall have some high-quality rock, there is also plenty of loose material, especially on new routes where the holds are untested. Strategies to mitigate this elevated risk include putting in ample protection, thoroughly testing holds, and rappelling to inspect and clean a new route from the top before committing to leading it from the bottom. (*Source: Banff, Yoho & Kootenay National Parks Visitor Safety Team.*)

HELICOPTER REQUESTED AT SUNSET | Inadequate Planning
Alberta, Banff National Park, Castle Mountain

A party of two climbers spent August 13 on Super Brewer, a long alpine rock climb that links the Ultra Brewer and Brewer Buttress routes on Castle Mountain. Ultra Brewer (330m, III 5.9) climbs to the Goat Plateau, a large ledge system at mid-height on the mountain, while Brewer Buttress (380m, II 5.6) continues to the top. A well-established yet fairly involved descent route follows a prominent gully with a few rappels to the Goat Plateau, and another series of rappels and downclimbing lead back to the base of the cliff.

Banff Dispatch received a call from an acquaintance of one of the climbers at 9:14 p.m., shortly after sunset. The caller had just talked to the subjects on their cell phone, and they reported they were still one pitch from the top. They had asked their acquaintance to call Parks Canada and arrange for them to be picked up from the top. Furthermore, they only had five percent battery life left on their phone.

Visitor Safety explained to the caller that it was too late for a helicopter to fly and requested the climbing party's phone number. The caller was asked not to contact the climbers again, so their remaining battery power could be used to communicate with Parks Canada.

Texts were sent to the subjects starting at 9:25 p.m. It was determined they had headlamps but did not know the usual climber's descent or the popular scrambling route down the opposite side of the mountain, and were using a topo stored on their phone for route information. The party was asked to decide whether they would attempt to descend or stay put. At 10:30 p.m., the party messaged back: "Too dark, we will stay here. Battery at 1%."

At this point, Visitor Safety made the decision to pick up the party first thing in the morning. This was not based on the party's request nor the expectation that they would have a rough night. Rather, there was no way to communicate with them. Further, even with good light and a route description in hand, many parties historically have had difficulty with this descent.

At 6:15 a.m. the next day, Visitor Safety personnel left Banff by helicopter. At 6:25 a.m., the party was found under their tarp, taking shelter in the lee of a rock outcrop directly above the top of the route. They were both adequately dressed and reported being a bit hungry and cold during the flight down to the highway.

ANALYSIS

The main problem facing this party was not knowing how to get down. If you plan to attempt a long, challenging route on a mountain, consider doing an easier route to learn the descent first. In this case, there were two viable descent options, but both would have been very difficult to figure out in the dark, and even more difficult with no route description or map. The party's decision to stay put was a good one.

The reliance on smart phones for communication, navigation, and a source of route information is becoming common. This tactic may work well on shorter, less-committing routes, but phones are less reliable on longer endeavors. As the device runs out of battery power, climbers are left with no communication resources at the most critical part of their day. Several strategies can be employed to prevent this situation:

- *Print hard copies of route information and maps.* Each party member should carry this information so the ability to make decisions in an emergency is not compromised. If all else fails, the paper can be used as a fire starter.
- *Carry alternate navigation tools, such as GPS or a compass.*
- *Carry a backup communication device.*
- *Preserve battery life.* If battery strength starts to get low, shut the device off. If your group is carrying two devices, keep the backup shut off. Alternatively, carry a backup battery supply to keep devices functioning.

This party had plenty of daylight when they arrived at the Goat Plateau, where they had easy access to the lower half of the descent route. The decision to continue on the upper route without being sure of the way down was a significant gamble. When the climbing day is not going as planned, communicate this fact early to an outside party. Communicate a clear set of intentions, and stick to that plan so outside resources do not have to guess what you will do. Organize check-in times so you can turn off communication devices to preserve battery life. Above all, do not wait until sunset to call for help. It is an unreasonable assumption to expect a rescue at night.

Finally, getting benighted does not need to be considered an emergency, as long as a party is prepared with the appropriate equipment. This party was well equipped with waterproof outerwear, warm layers, and a tarp. They made a good decision not to attempt an unfamiliar descent in the dark, but with a written route description in their pockets, they likely could have safely descended in the morning for a big breakfast in Banff. (*Source: Banff, Yoho & Kootenay National Parks Visitor Safety Team.*)

LEADER FALL | Protection Pulled Out
Alberta, Banff National Park, Mt. Louis

On August 28, an experienced party set out to climb Homage to the Spider (5.10a) on Mt. Louis, near Banff. The route is an alpine rock climb with a three-hour approach. It starts with a few hundred meters of third- and fourth-class scrambling to reach a bolted anchor. From this anchor, there is a short descent into a gully, where the technical rock climbing starts.

The first pitch is 5.9 and includes a corner that is often dirty or wet. The leader started up this first pitch and made an extra effort to place some pieces in the lower part of the pitch. The upper part consists of a wide crack that can be protected with number 4 cams. In an effort to keep packs light, the climbers had brought only a single number 4, intending to bump that cam up the wide section. The leader had climbed the route several times before and felt comfortable with this tactic.

High on the pitch, the leader set the big cam and committed to the final moves up to the anchor. During a layback move, one foot slipped and the climber started falling. The number 4 cam pulled out of the rock, and the climber kept falling before being stopped by a smaller cam lower down. The climber's body contacted some ledgy terrain, and at least one ankle was broken. The belayer lowered the injured leader to the bottom of the climb, and the party called for help using their Satellite Emergency Notification Device (SEND).

Banff Visitor Safety personnel responded via helicopter and assessed the scene. The gully where the patient was located was too tight for helicopter access, but rescuers were able to move the injured climber and partner to the anchor above the pitch, from which the climbers and rescuers could be slung out to a staging area in the valley below.

ANALYSIS

The leader was very experienced and had climbed Homage to the Spider six times. The route and gear requirements were known in detail. The leader also had a lot of experience placing trad gear and

Helicopter slinging injured climber to a staging area in the Gargoyle Valley between Mt. Louis and Mt. Edith. *Parks Canada* described the number 4 cam that pulled as "90 percent good." In hindsight, the leader thought the cam pulled out because the sides of the crack were coated with fine dirt and limestone dust. Meltwater from snow high up on the route funnels down the corner on pitch one, and this pitch is always covered in varying degrees of dirt. The leader felt that dirt on the sides of the crack decreased the friction between the cam lobes and the rock.

This is a common problem on alpine routes and even more so in winter with ice and water ever present. Cams are highly suspect if the friction of the cam lobes on the rock is inadequate. Passive protection that has a tighter fit—such as nuts, hexes, or pitons hammered into cracks—might inspire more confidence when the friction of the side walls is an issue.

On previous ascents of this route, the leader often did not place the smaller cam that actually caught the fall. The leader made an effort to place more protection this time and was very glad to have done so. That small cam had been deemed a much worse placement than the large cam that pulled out—but you never know what can happen.

From a rescuer perspective, there was concern regarding rockfall from the party overhead. As a general rule, if you are above an accident scene, stop moving while a rescue is in process. If you are not moving, the chance of knocking rocks onto the scene below is greatly reduced. (*Source: Banff, Yoho & Kootenay National Parks Visitor Safety Team.*)

LEADER FALL | Loose Rock, No Belay, Possible Haste
Alberta, Banff National Park, Mt. Rundle Traverse

On July 20, a party of three made their second attempt to traverse Mt. Rundle from Canmore to Banff. They had attempted the traverse earlier in the summer and made it to a bivy site just beneath Peak 7. They aborted the attempt at that time because the traverse was too snowy, making for slow travel. They monitored the peak and made their second attempt after a period of good weather that melted away the alpine snow, leaving the ridge in dry condition.

The Mt. Rundle Traverse covers about 25 kilometers and passes over 11 separate summits. The technical difficulty is about 5.5, but loose rock and the sheer length of the traverse compound the difficulties. The complete traverse usually requires at least one very long day.

In the afternoon, the party reached Peak 10, which has a short chimney climb right below its summit. At this rock step, one of the party members (E.M.) wanted a belay. A.S. offered to drag a rope up to the top, set up an anchor, and belay E.M. up. A.S. was about 20 meters up, comfortably climbing the chimney, when a foothold broke and the climber fell to the ledge below, breaking one lower leg. A.S. was not on belay at the time of the fall, so E.M. pulled in the slack and wrapped the rope around her hands. This makeshift belay and the rope running around a large, loose boulder blocked A.S. from tumbling further down the west side of Mt. Rundle.

Immediately after the fall, at 2:45 p.m., the party requested a rescue with their inReach device. Parks Canada rescue personnel were able to communicate with the climbers on their cell phone briefly, but the phone battery was low, and cell communication ended abruptly. At 3:45 p.m., two rescue personnel heli-slung into the acci-

Peak 10 of the Rundle Traverse, showing the chimney where a climber fell. *dowclimbing.com*

dent site, placed a bolt to secure personnel and party members, administered first aid, and slung the patient down to the awaiting ambulance.

ANALYSIS

Members of the party were in their 20s and had moved to the Bow Valley a year and a half prior to attempting the Mt. Rundle Traverse. They had approximately four years of mountaineering experience in Scotland and some locally. They were properly equipped with technical climbing equipment and were well prepared to call for rescue.

Loose rock is common in the Rockies. Carefully selecting and testing handholds and footholds is a common strategy to prevent a fall. The consequences of the fall may have been minimized if the lead climber had been belayed and was able to place protection. Likely, the desire to move quickly through this passage, with another technical peak and a long descent still to go, contributed to the decision to climb unbelayed. (*Source: Banff, Yoho & Kootenay National Parks Visitor Safety Team.*)

FALL ON ROCK | Inadequate Belay
Alberta, Bow Valley, Grassi Lakes

On August 26, an experienced, 38-year-old, male climber was leading an unknown sport route on Gardener's Wall at Grassi Lakes. The climber fell about 40 feet to the ground after the belayer lost control of the rope. During the fall, the climber hit a ledge and sustained multiple injuries, including fractures of the 12th thoracic vertebra and pelvis, a dislocated ankle, and an open fracture of the lower leg. He was heli-slung from the scene to emergency medical services. It was reported that he was expected to recover in six months.

ANALYSIS

In a newspaper story, the injured climber was quoted as saying, "I had clipped the last bolt and I could see the anchor, but I was getting tired because of the routes we did just before. I was about six feet from the anchor and realized I wouldn't make it. I called to [the belayer] below me to say that I was going to fall, so she could be prepared to help stop the fall. She didn't hear me. I started to free fall, pulling the rope off her hand. She tried to grab the rope with her free hand, but I was heavier and it was more force on her." The story said the belayer suffered third-degree burns on one hand.

This pair had climbed together "often," and it is not known what caused the belayer to lose control of the rope, but a belayer must be prepared to catch a fall at any moment. (*Sources: Matt Mueller, public safety specialist, and Kamsack Times.*)

ROCKFALL | Poor Position
Alberta, Bow Valley, Grotto Mountain

Jughaul Wall is a three-pitch Bow Valley trad classic. I'd climbed it without incident three times over the past 18 years. This time, as I neared the top of the first pitch (5.5), I saw two shiny new bolts above a small ledge. I assumed this was where the pitch ended and set up the belay for the second pitch there. When my partner, Tibor, was about four meters up on the second pitch (5.7), I suddenly remembered that when I'd climbed this route before, we had ended the first pitch in an alcove higher up.

When Tibor was approximately 40 meters up, he stepped on a ledge that failed, resulting in significant rockfall. Several pieces the size of bread loaves bounded down the face and directly onto my exposed belay stance. Fortunately, I was hit only by five smaller rocks, which resulted in various flesh wounds. We rappelled off, patched a bleeding leg wound with a gauze pad and duct tape, and walked back to the car under our own steam. In retrospect, I was just plain lucky. Although I was wearing a helmet, a direct head hit by one of the big rocks likely would have been fatal.

ANALYSIS

We got into trouble because we did not consider my belay stance's exposure to potential rockfall. If we had relocated the belay for the second pitch to the well-protected alcove I had used before, I would not have been injured by the rockfall.

The new bolts that I mistakenly took to be the belay station for the second pitch may have been placed for rappelling the route. The walk-off from this route is tedious, so rapping to descend has definite appeal. But this new station is exposed to rockfall for anyone who rappels the route or chooses to belay from this spot.

Ice climbers are very careful about where they set up belays, because falling ice is a given. From now on, I'll give a lot more thought to where I belay when rock climbing. (*Source: Everett Fee.*)

FALL ON ROCK | Inadequate Protection
Alberta, Bow Valley, Yamnuska

A party of three was climbing Grillmair Chimneys, an eight-pitch 5.6 route on Yamnuska, on May 24. When the leader fell on pitch three, the rope dragged over a rock rib separating two gullies and the sheath was cut, exposing the core. The leader broke one arm during the fall. When rescuers arrived, the three climbers were asked via text to rappel one pitch to a ledge that was easier for rescue crews to access. A rescue team member was dropped off by helicopter, and the injured climber was belayed to the rescuer's location and then heli-slung to the base.

ANALYSIS

Further details on the leader's fall were not available. It can be assumed the leader placed inadequate protection, and that this lengthened his fall. A report suggested that rope drag might have been an issue, and perhaps long slings could have mitigated both the drag and the sheath damage. (*Matt Mueller, public safety specialist, Alberta Parks.*)

MEXICO

LEDGE COLLAPSE | Severed Rope
Chihuahua, Basaseachic Falls National Park, El Gigante

On March 6, my best friend Nolan Smythe, 26, and I were on the second day of a free ascent of Logical Progression, a 28-pitch 5.13 big-wall sport climb on El Gigante. Nolan was leading pitch 14. The sun had just gone down, and we had two moderate 5.11 pitches to go before our next bivy. He made it about 80 feet into the pitch and then, after manteling onto a large ledge, the refrigerator-size block of volcanic rock dislodged from under his feet. As he was falling, the rope was cut by the huge block and he fell all the way to the ground.

I was left alone on the wall with a shortened lead line and a limited number of draws. A three-day storm was forecast to start the next afternoon. Below me was a sizable traverse that I wasn't confident I'd be able to descend safely while keeping my bivy kit. On top of that, we had rappelled in to start the climb, and I didn't know the walk-out exit for the canyon; this exit route also passes very near several poppy fields run by the local cartel.

Instead, I started roped soloing up to our planned bivy. I primarily used a stick clip, but on occasion free climbing was necessary. I alerted a good friend, Sergio "Tiny" Almada, about the situation via my inReach, and he started toward the wall with another Mexican climber, José David "Bicho" Martinez, planning to rappel in so I could jumar the last 1,200 feet to the top. They arrived as the rain started, and we left my kit behind to jug out quickly. We returned a week later, after the body recovery, and cleaned all of my gear off the wall.

ANALYSIS

All told, this seemed like a freak accident more than anything else. I recall rappelling past the same ledge earlier with a large haul bag. It looked concerning, but after giving it a thorough test, I deemed it solid. Nolan must have had the same thoughts during his lead. It had been snowing for three days before we rappelled in, and this accident happened three days after the snow stopped. It is possible that a freeze-thaw cycle contributed to the rockfall, but there is no way of definitively knowing. Sometimes a rock that many people have pulled on has a day that it is going to release. Unfortunately, it released on Nolan.

Don't underestimate Logical Progression because it's a "sport route." This wall is remote, large, and committing. The weather can be really bad. Be prepared. You are on your own out there—help in case of an accident isn't as close as you think it is in Chihuahua.

We were prepared with bivy gear, a stick clip, extra draws, an inReach, and the knowledge to go up or down the wall safely on our own. Nolan and I were both well within our comfort level. We both had quickly dispatched the first 5.13 pitch on the route on the morning of the accident. Some accidents are simply a matter of being in the wrong place at the wrong time. (*Source: Aaron Livingston.*)

A skier triggered a slide above this cliff band near Alpental in Washington. He went over the rocks and was buried below. Two partners located the injured skier and dug him out. *Northwest Avalanche Center*

BACKCOUNTRY AVALANCHES

This section examines a selection of U.S. avalanche accidents involving backcountry skiers and snowboarders. These incidents occurred during the most recent winter season, from December 2020 through April 2021. They were selected to cover a variety of accident types and are arranged geographically. Unless otherwise noted, the narratives and analyses have been adapted from reports originally published by regional avalanche centers, and were reviewed by the centers for accuracy.

SIDECOUNTRY AVALANCHE | Unaware of Forecast
Washington, Mt. Baker-Snoqualmie National Forest, Alpental Valley

In the afternoon of Saturday, April 10, 2021, a group of three skiers loaded Chair 2 at Alpental ski area to access terrain beyond the area boundary. They had been skiing inbounds in the Alpental back bowls for a large part of the day. Upon reaching Piss Pass, the trio ascended on foot to the top of a small knob (5,440 feet) separating the Alpental resort and the Pineapple Pass area. While the team discussed the intended route, they did not discuss that the line was in the backcountry, nor had anyone in the group checked the avalanche forecast for the area. Only some of the skiers carried avalanche rescue gear, and they had varying degrees of formal avalanche instruction.

Skier 1 led the group off the knob and toward a run known as 261. The group witnessed a lone snowboarder riding a line very close to their intended descent. Prior to entering the run, Skier 1 mentioned the possibility of wind slabs on the slope and the presence of a cliff below them and to the left.

At approximately 4:30 p.m., Skier 1 traveled onto a slope just to skier's left of 261 and triggered an avalanche. He yelled to his friends and pointed his skis downhill, skied directly over the cliff he had observed, and landed on the slopes below. While Skier 1 attempted to keep his airway clear, the avalanche immediately began to bury him.

Skiers 2 and 3 were above and out of the main start zone when the slide released. They quickly did a visual search of the terrain above the cliff and then descended a sparsely treed area to the north of the avalanche. Once they arrived below the cliff, they visually searched the debris field and found a ski pole on the surface and the tip of a ski sticking out of the snow just downhill.

Skier 3 began assembling his avalanche shovel and instructed Skier 2 to begin digging with his hands in the direction of the victim's head. They very quickly uncovered a hand that allowed them to locate and uncover Skier 1's face. He was attempting to yell, but his airway was clogged with snow. From the time the avalanche released to clearing the victim's airway was less than five minutes. Skier 1 was lying on his back, with his head approximately 18 inches below the surface. Despite the relatively shallow burial, he could not move nor extricate himself.

After uncovering their teammate, the group recognized the potential overhead hazard from additional avalanches and chose to move. Despite his injuries—the skier had two broken bones in his left shoulder and a torn ACL—he was able to slide down-valley to a flat area. At this point, skier 1's knee injury made further travel challenging.

No one in the team had cell service. Skier 3 left the group to descend to the ski area and seek help, while Skier 2 remained with the patient. Alpental Patrol was notified at about 5:15 p.m. and responded to the scene. They were able to load Skier 1 into a sled and extricate him to the base of the ski resort.

ANALYSIS

In a forecast issued at 6:43 p.m. on April 9, the evening before this incident, the avalanche danger above and near treeline was rated Considerable on all aspects. The summary that evening read: "Another potent storm will impact Snoqualmie Pass, resulting in dangerous avalanche conditions on Saturday. Unstable snow, recent human-triggered avalanches, and dynamic springtime weather should lead you to dial back your terrain choices and avoid slopes over 35 degrees."

Alpental Patrol and Northwest Avalanche Center (NWAC) staff visited the site the next day to complete an investigation. They found that a soft slab avalanche had begun on northwest-facing slope with a start zone averaging 40°. The crown was 10 to 12 inches deep, and the slide was about 150 feet wide and ran 350 vertical feet. In a pit, the investigators found that 10 to 12 inches of storm snow from the night before had slid on a thin layer of small facets. A storm the previous Wednesday night had delivered up to 16 inches of snow near Snoqualmie Pass, along with strong winds.

The NWAC forecast from the evening before this incident reported, "On Friday, multiple skier-triggered avalanches occurred at Snoqualmie Pass, including an involvement where a skier was caught and carried." The report continued, "As we navigate our way through springtime weather, the transitions between dry and wet avalanche problems can be rapid and unpredictable, just like the weather. It can make decision-making and forecasting challenging, since you can't bring your winter mindset or spring mindset to the mountains to rely on for any given day." (Source: Northwest Avalanche Center.)

RESORT ACCESS TO THE BACKCOUNTRY: *Before skiers and riders leave a resort through a backcountry access gate, they need to flip a mental switch and acknowledge they are entering unpatrolled slopes with all the hazards of backcountry travel, requiring all appropriate training and rescue gear. Sidecountry skiing and riding (resort-accessed backcountry touring) accounted for about 10 percent of all U.S. avalanche fatalities over the last decade.*

FATAL BURIAL | Faulty Transceiver
California, Klamath National Forest, Etna Summit

A backcountry skier and snowboarder were caught in an avalanche near Etna Summit, about 40 miles west of Mt. Shasta, at approximately 2 p.m. on February 3, 2021. Both individuals had many years of backcountry experience, carried avalanche rescue gear, and were familiar with the area.

The avalanche occurred shortly after they reached the top of their intended descent route (immediately below a ridgeline) and were preparing to descend. Both riders were carried down the slope by the slide. The skier was pinned and buried against a tree within 20 to 30 feet. The snowboarder was swept through the trees and partially buried some distance down the slope.

The snowboarder extracted himself and immediately began a transceiver search, but the device malfunctioned. At this point, he began to dig in the most likely burial location and exposed a ski pole, which led to the buried victim. Approximately 25 to 30 minutes had passed between the burial and extrication. The survivor performed CPR for over an hour, but was unable to revive his partner.

ANALYSIS
The avalanche occurred at 6,650 feet on a northwest aspect, near treeline and just below a ridge. The slope was 35 to 39 degrees. A hard wind slab up to two feet thick was triggered; the avalanche measured 70 feet wide and slid about 200 vertical feet.

The area had received "feet" of new snow in the previous couple of weeks. A few days of sun had helped consolidate the storm snow. On February 3, the day of the accident, an observer found 8 to 10 inches of fresh snow at a similar elevation in the Mt. Eddy area, 25 miles to the east, with moderate northwest wind and blowing snow.

The party had performed a transceiver check in the parking lot before they began their tour. Both transceivers appeared to be functioning and had good battery life. However, further investigation found a corroded battery compartment in the transceiver, which likely led to the malfunction. (*Source: Mount Shasta Avalanche Center.*)

CLEAN YOUR BEACONS

Corrosion in the battery compartment of transceivers is an insidious hazard, because the transceiver may function perfectly one minute and fail the next. Never leave batteries in the transceiver through the summer or for long in-season layoffs. (You should always install fresh batteries at the start of the season.) Avoid situations that allow moisture or condensation to get into the compartment. Inspect the batteries and contracts periodically. If you find corrosion (usually a whitish powder), gently clean it off with a Q-tip and rubbing alcohol or vinegar, a pencil eraser, or by snapping the batteries in and out of position to loosen the foreign material. Take care not to damage the contacts. If the battery contacts cannot be cleaned, contact the manufacturer.

SLAB TRIGGERED WHILE SKINNING | Perceived 'Safer' Area
Utah, Wasatch Mountains, Mill Creek Canyon

On the morning of February 6, 2021, two different groups (eight people total) went to ski the Wilson Glades, a north-facing, 500-foot run just below the 9,950-foot summit of Wilson Peak. On the day of the accident, the avalanche danger was rated as High for northeast-facing terrain above 9,500 feet.

Chris, Sarah, Louis, Thomas, and Steve (Group A) approached from Big Cottonwood Canyon. While ascending Wilson Peak, Group A noticed a very large natural avalanche in the Wilson Chutes on the east side of the peak. They posted a photo of this avalanche on Instagram and tagged the Utah Avalanche Center at 8:33 a.m. At the top, they discussed how to ski Wilson Glades but never discussed if they should ski it or not. They discussed avoiding the steeper sections and going one at a time, with everyone participating in that discussion. Once the group reached the bottom of the Wilson Glades, they started breaking a trail back to the top to ski again.

Nate, Ethan, and Steph (Group B) approached from Mill Creek Canyon, starting at 8:30 a.m. Group B saw several natural avalanches in Alexander Basin while ascending their route into the Wilson Glades. Group B was aware that the avalanche danger was rated High and that Wilson Glades could avalanche. Their general plan for the day was to avoid avalanche terrain, and their specific travel plan was to stop at some point before the steeper section, and discuss where to go and what to ski. Ethan and Steph were familiar with the area, while it was Nate's first time skiing the Wilson Glades. Neither group dug a snow pit to investigate the snowpack.

Group B reached the bottom of Wilson Glades and noted many ski tracks and a recent skin track, which they started to follow uphill. When Nate and Ethan reached a point where they could see the steeper slopes above them, they waited in a sparse opening in the trees for Steph.

Group A skied the Wilson Glades a total of three times. After their second lap, Steve opted to wait above. Following the third lap, they began ascending with the intent to finish the day by skiing back to the trailhead in Big Cottonwood Canyon. At the steepest part of their track, they regrouped at a large tree to cross the final slope one at a time. Chris went first. He reported hearing something that sounded like an earthquake. The avalanche broke approximately 30 feet above them, and Sarah, Thomas, and Louis were swept downhill. Chris lunged for a tree and hit it so hard that the "wind was knocked out of him." Both skis were ripped off his feet, and he was left hanging *above* the bed surface after the avalanche passed. (It is very unusual that someone can hang onto a tree in an avalanche as Chris did.)

As Group A was caught in the avalanche, Ethan and Nate (Group B) looked up and saw a wall of snow coming at them. Nate initially thought the avalanche would not reach them, but then remembers the snow overtaking him and Ethan and being buried as the debris stopped moving. He quickly lost consciousness.

Chris dropped out of the tree and screamed for Steve, on the ridge above, to come down. Chris turned his transceiver to receive and began searching downhill on foot in a zigzag pattern. Chris acquired a transceiver signal, deployed his avalanche probe, and quickly located a person. Chris and Steve dug down four to six feet and uncovered Nate—someone they didn't know—who was unconscious but breathing.

then located and uncovered Ethan a few feet away and at the same depth– another skier they were surprised to see. Ethan, too, was unconscious but breathing. At 11:40 a.m., Chris called 911 and provided brief details about the avalanche and location.

Chris then acquired another transceiver signal approximately 150 feet to the east. Chris, Steve, and Nate (who by then had joined the search) located and uncovered Sarah, Louis, and Thomas in succession; they were buried approximately 30 feet apart down the fall line at a depth of four to six feet. None was breathing or had a pulse, and after attempting CPR on Sarah, no further lifesaving measures were taken.

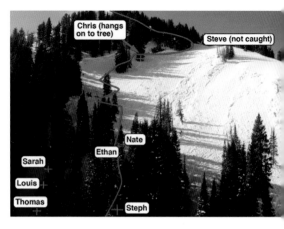

Position of eight skiers after the Wilson Glades avalanche. (The skin track is shown in red.) All but one of them were skinning up the slope when the slide occurred. *Utah Avalanche Center*

Chris and Steve then acquired a signal 100 feet to the west. They found Steph buried about six feet deep. She was likewise not breathing and did not have a pulse.

By the time all six people had been dug out of the debris (two alive and four deceased), multiple helicopters were circling above with rescue personnel on board. Chris, Nate, Ethan, and Steve were hoisted off the scene. With darkness approaching, operations were discontinued until the following day, when recovery efforts were completed.

ANALYSIS

The Wilson Glades have seen many close calls. It is perceived as relatively safe compared with nearby areas, because it is less steep. It seldom avalanches naturally; as in this incident, slides seem more often human triggered.

Analysis of the crown profile revealed the slide was caused by a four-inch-thick weak layer of faceted snow formed during periods of cold, dry weather. It was buried three feet deep under the hard slab that failed. The crown was nearly 1,000 feet wide. The slope angle where the crown profile was recorded was 31 degrees, as was the slope where most of the ski tracks from Group A were located. Their uphill skin track was a touch steeper. Any slope above 30 degrees is considered avalanche terrain.

All the skiers except Chis had one or both skis still attached to their feet when they were buried, which may have contributed to deeper burials. Because they were all skinning uphill, the toe pieces of their bindings were likely in the walking or locked position, making it diffcult for the skis to release from their feet. In a study of avalanche fatalities in the U.S. between 2009 and 2017, avalanche forecaster Evelyn Lees found that 32 percent of fatalities among tourers happened during the ascent. Her study stresses the need to find safe ascent routes.

Chris and Steve saved two lives (Nate and Ethan), and Chris, Nate, and Steve gave their best attempt to save the rest. Their rescue efforts were top-notch, and they knew how to perform companion rescue quickly and efficiently. They did the absolute best anyone could do with six full burials. (*Source: Utah Avalanche Center.*)

CARRIED DOWN STEEP COULOIR | Terrain Trap
Wyoming, Grand Teton National Park, Broken Thumb Couloir

On February 22, 2021, a group of two splitboarders and one skier toured from Taggart Lake trailhead up 25 Short (so named because the peak is 25 feet short of 10,000) to descend the Broken Thumb Couloir into Avalanche Canyon. This is a very narrow chute, and the descent normally involves a 50- to 100-foot rappel in the lower half.

A little after 11 a.m., a 33-year-old rider was leading the group down through steep trees and rocky terrain to the entrance of the couloir when he triggered an avalanche that carried him down the confined, rocky couloir and over the rappel zone. He was carried about 800 vertical feet and stopped by a tree, suffering significant trauma, and was buried. His friends located him with a transceiver but could not revive him.

The avalanche was a recent wind slab estimated at 150 to 200 feet wide and two feet deep at the maximum. It ran 1,100 vertical feet. This relatively small avalanche occurred directly above steep, rocky, and vertical terrain and took the snowboarder on an unsurvivable fall.

ANALYSIS
All the individuals involved in this incident had at least a Level 1 avalanche class and significant experience in avalanche terrain.

Beginning February 12, snow fell daily in this area up to February 22, with an estimated 65 inches recorded at the Surprise Meadow snow station, about two miles north of the accident site. In the week prior, many avalanches were reported in Grand Teton National Park. The Bridger-Teton Avalanche Center's hazard rating for February 22 was Considerable (Level 3 out of 5).

This accident occurred on serious terrain above a large cliff. Due to the exposure, this was not only an avalanche accident but also a mountaineering accident. Two other avalanche fatalities happened in the Bridger-Teton forecast area earlier in the same week, and all of them occurred in steep terrain exposed to terrain traps.

On February 17, a group of nine snowmobilers was riding in the Salt River Range, southeast of Alpine, when a soft slab avalanche caught seven members of the party. Two were buried and rescued, but one was swept with his sled into a treed area at the base of the slope and was buried in four to five feet of debris.

On February 18, a group six snowboarders built a jump above a steep bank in the backcountry near Togwotee Pass. A 31-year-male made the first jump and triggered a slab avalanche on the 42-degree bank. He was carried to the creek bottom at the base of the bank and was buried under nine feet of avalanche debris.

When natural and human-triggered avalanches are happening, terrain selection is essential. (*Source: Bridger-Teton Avalanche Center.*)

TRIGGERED SLAB | Inconsistent Snow Depth
Montana, Absaroka Range, Republic Mountain

On the morning of January 8, 2021, a group of six skiers (one female and five males) met in Cooke City and decided to ski the Fin on Republic Mountain. None of them had been to this particular slope or mountain before. All members carried an avalanche transceiver, shovel, and probe, and three were wearing helmets. Two carried avalanche airbag packs. All had at least some avalanche education. They had read the local avalanche forecast the day before, but not the day of this incident (the danger had not changed).

On their ascent, visibility was poor and they could not see the entire slope or the ridgeline they intended to climb. As they left the trees, they dug two pits and performed [stability] tests. One later wrote, "Though we identified potential weak layers at 60 cm and a deeper one... we got minimal failure and no propagation. What we saw in the pits was a nice right-side-up snowpack. However, we knew if we skinned along the ridge to the southwest, the snowpack would

Avalanche on the Fin of Republic Mountain. The skiers' skin track can be seen at right. The fracture they triggered propagated upward for 250 feet. The slide swept three skiers into the trees. *Gallatin National Forest Avalanche Center*

change due to wind exposure. We discussed mitigating this by skinning close to the ridge and skiing back down our skin track if we saw warning signs."

As they continued and "when those in the skin track crossed over a wind lip into a slightly more southerly aspect," they felt the slope collapse and watched a crack propagate 250 feet upslope. The avalanche broke 1.5 to two feet deep, 200 feet wide, and ran 700 feet vertically. Skiers 1 and 2 were carried the full distance to the base of the slope. Skier 3 was carried about midway downslope. Skier 4 was at the edge of the slide and able to hold their position, and Skiers 5 and 6 were further back in the skin track.

Skier 1 deployed his airbag and was partially buried. He freed himself from the debris and began a transceiver search. He followed the signal to Skier 2, whose head was buried more than two feet deep; the skier was unconscious and not breathing. Skier 1 cleared Skier 2's airway, and Skier 2 began breathing and regained consciousness. Skier 2 sustained injuries to his leg, but later made it out under his own power.

Skiers 4, 5, and 6 quickly skied down to help Skier 3, who was partially buried about halfway down the slide path and sustained serious injuries to his ribs and lungs. Skiers 4 and 6 had two-way radios and called for help. (There is no cell service in this region.) They were able to contact someone with a radio in Cooke City, who reported it to Park County Search and Rescue. Because Skier 3 could not move, the group eventually congregated at Skier 3's position, where they built a fire and waited for rescuers. Skier 3 was evacuated by helicopter at about 4 p.m., and the rest of the party was able to get out under their own power with the help of rescuers.

ANALYSIS

The avalanche occurred on an east aspect at 9,700 feet. The average slope angle was 37 degrees (33 degrees at the crown). The mountains near Cooke City had received heavy snow in October and November, which formed a dense, two- to four-foot-deep snowpack on many slopes. In late November to December, minimal snowfall and cold temperatures led to the formation of weak layers of sugary facets on some slopes, especially where the snowpack was relatively shallow. These layers were buried by subsequent heavy snowfall in late December, followed by small storms through the first week of January.

The skiers dug a six-foot-deep snow pit close to where the avalanche was triggered. They found good snow structure and good stability in their pit, which investigators confirmed the next day when they dug in the same spot. Approximately 100 feet away, with a slight change in aspect, the snowpack thinned from six feet to two to three feet deep. This thin area is where they initiated a fracture in the faceted grains.

In a video produced at the accident scene and in comments to viewers, Doug Chabot of Gallatin National Forest Avalanche Center said the snowpack was mostly six feet or deeper in the mountains around Cooke City at the time, but thinned in places at higher elevations and among rocky terrain. "Be really careful and paying attention to if the snowpack is changing as you're skinning along," he said. "As soon as [these skiers] wrapped around to a slightly different aspect, the depth and snow structure changed. A stability test is one of many pieces of info that goes into deciding whether to ski or not. A poor test result is enough to turn around, yet the absence of that is not a green light to move forward. Other things have to be going your way to give your decision weight.... The bottom line is that you should know that the snow is very stable if you are considering entering large, highly consequential avalanche terrain like the Fin." (*Source: Gallatin National Forest Avalanche Center.*)

CHANGE OF PLANS | Inadequate Equipment
Colorado, Crested Butte Area, Snodgrass Mountain

At midday on December 15, Rider 1 and Skier 2, a married couple and Crested Butte residents, left for a short tour. Rider 1 traveled on a splitboard, while Skier 2 was on lightweight touring skis. Since their plan was to ski up and descend the snow-covered Snodgrass Road, with no exposure to avalanche terrain, they chose not to bring their avalanche rescue equipment.

At the top of the road, they changed plans and decided to descend much steeper terrain off Snodgrass Mountain to the north. A friend had traveled off the north side the day prior and reported great conditions. The couple recognized they were ill-equipped for travel in avalanche terrain, but they proceeded.

From near the summit, they descended a steep, forested slope. Travel through the weak, faceted snowpack was difficult, and they hit many rocks and stumps. They descended about 1,000 vertical feet and arrived at the top of an open slope around 10,000 feet in elevation. Skier 2 watched while Rider 1 descended first. He made one turn and the slope avalanched. He was pulled into the flowing snow, and Skier 2 quickly lost sight of him.

The avalanche flowed through a band of small trees. Rider 1 was slammed into a four- to five-inch-diameter tree, and the impact broke his leg. Rider 1 was wrapped around the tree, unburied, and alert when the avalanche stopped.

Skier 2 followed her husband's track onto the bed surface of the avalanche and carefully switchbacked down until she heard him call out and skied straight to his position lower on the slope. He was bleeding significantly and unable to walk. Despite poor cell coverage, Skier 2 was able to place a call to 911 at 2:26 p.m. A medical helicopter was able to land near the toe of the avalanche and pick up Rider 1 at about 4 p.m.

ANALYSIS

The soft slab avalanche broke on a layer of faceted snow capped by a thin layer of surface hoar, and it released broadly: about 300 feet across the full width of this small avalanche path. The extent of propagation for such a soft slab hints at the very weak nature of the snow below it. As the avalanche ran, it scoured most of the snow down to a buried sun crust. Debris piled up to three feet deep.

An early season avalanche on Snodgrass Mountain (triggered at circle) scoured a small, steep path and slammed a snowboarder into a tree (X). *Colorado Avalanche Information Center*

The Colorado Avalanche Information Center's Gunnison zone rated the hazard as Considerable (Level 3 out of 5) near and above treeline, and Moderate (Level 2) below treeline. The CAIC recorded 186 avalanches in the Gunnison zone between December 10 and 14. Seventeen of the avalanches were triggered by people on below-treeline, northeast-facing slopes similar to the accident slope.

This couple made a last-minute decision to enter avalanche terrain without detailed knowledge of the terrain. (Rider 1 had ridden down the north side of Snodgrass three times before, while Skier 2 had not.) After a few minutes of descending, they recognized that they had underestimated the steepness and complexity of the terrain. Reflecting afterward, they described not knowing how to fix the situation they had created. Turning around and skinning to the ridge did not occur to them at the time, but it might have been the best solution.

Rider 1 was not buried and was very lucky that getting caught did not have much worse consequences. It's a great reminder to always carry avalanche rescue equipment in the winter backcountry. (*Source: Colorado Avalanche Information Center.*)

BURIED AT BASE OF RUN | Waiting for Partner in Runout Zone
Colorado, East Vail

On February 4 at around 11:10 a.m., two skiers were caught by an avalanche in an area east of the Vail resort known locally as Marvin's West or Big Marvin. This is a steep, east-facing slope below treeline that is dissected by two cliff bands in the avalanche start zone.

Skiers 1 and 2 had exited the Vail ski area through a backcountry access gate around 10:15 a.m. They hiked east for about 30 minutes and then descended along the ridgeline to the north to reach the top of the large, open bowl of Marvin's West. They arrived at around 10:55 a.m.

Skier 1 made his way down through a series of cliff bands to a bench about 800 vertical feet below the ridge and waited there for Skier 2. The second skier began her descent and skied about 300 vertical feet, down to a narrow opening through a cliff band, and then triggered a large avalanche that broke above her. She tried to escape to the trees and managed to stay upright, and she came to a stop on the apron below the cliff band, buried to her knees in avalanche debris.

Skier 2 descended the debris field, observing that Skier 1 was not at their rendez-vous point and that the avalanche had run well past the bench where he was supposed to be waiting. She switched her transceiver to receive and headed in the direction of the rendezvous point. Skier 2 located her partner and began digging. Skier 1 was found buried 2.5 to 3 feet deep. Skier 2 cleared the snow from around his head and shoulders. He was not breathing. This was about 10 minutes after the avalanche.

Skier 2 called Vail Ski Patrol at 11:20 a.m. to report the accident. Three other side-country tourers were riding in an area just east of Marvin's West. They made their way to the scene, where they helped dig Skier 1 from the avalanche debris. One of the riders called Vail Ski Patrol, reported that CPR was in progress, and sent the dispatcher the coordinates. About an hour later, before patrollers could reach the scene, the skiers and riders decided that further resuscitation efforts would not be effective.

ANALYSIS

The Colorado Avalanche Information Center (CAIC) had issued an Avalanche Warning for the Vail/Summit County zone at 6 a.m. on February 4, the day of the accident. The warning read, in part, "A foot or more of new snow and strong winds have combined to overload our fragile snowpack. Large, wide, and deadly avalanches will be very easy to trigger. Natural avalanches can run long distances." CAIC's forecast for this zone rated the avalanche danger at High near and above treeline and Considerable below treeline.

Extended periods of dry weather in November, December, and the first half of January had created a weak base for the snowpack. In the five days before the accident, about two feet of snow fell, including 12 inches in the 24 hours preceding the incident. Westerly to northwesterly winds had transported new snow to east-facing slopes throughout the night.

The soft slab avalanche unintentionally triggered by Skier 2 broke about two to three feet deep (into old snow layers). It was 700 feet wide and ran about 1,000 vertical feet. The slope angle was 38 degrees.

Skiers 1 and 2 made their plan to ski Marvin's West based on previous experience in the terrain. Skier 1 stopped in a place he felt was safe because he had never seen an avalanche run that far, and because it was a common rendezvous point for people who frequent the East Vail backcountry. Travel habits developed during usual conditions do not always work during periods when avalanches are breaking wider and running further than you have previously witnessed.

Vegetation and terrain can be more reliable than recent memory to determine safer areas. Look for the trim lines of the avalanche path—these are the areas where

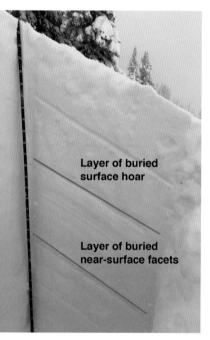

Layer of buried surface hoar

Layer of buried near-surface facets

Snow profile observed near the top of Marvin's West a day after the slide. Forecasters found two weak layers in the upper 100 cm (39 inches) of snowpack. *Colorado Avalanche Information Center*

larger trees are still standing. You can also look for trees that are flagged, with all of the uphill branches ripped off by successive avalanches. In the area where Skier 1 was waiting, there are only small, sparse trees. The trim lines are far away, which means that historically avalanches have overrun this area. In the early 1990s, an avalanche here ran the entire way to the valley bottom and put debris on Interstate 70.

Safe travel techniques include regrouping outside of avalanche run-out zones, particularly when large avalanches are likely. In some situations, that may mean leap-frogging your partner in small sections, or deciding not to travel through a specific area because there are no safe places to regroup. In this particular avalanche path, there are not many safe places to stop and regroup, and it is not a safe place to be when the avalanche danger is Considerable. (*Source: Colorado Avalanche Information Center.*)

VERY LARGE AVALANCHE | Riding Alone, Inadequate Gear
Colorado, Front Range, Mt. Trelease

Just after 8 a.m. on February 14, 2021, Rider 1 parked at the trailhead for Mt. Trelease and noticed one car already in the parking area. As Rider 1 ascended the skin track, he deduced there was one backcountry tourer ahead of him (Rider 2), based on the tracks in the fresh snow. At about 9 a.m., Rider 1 got his first view of Pat's Knob, a steep slope on the east side of Mt. Trelease, and saw the aftermath of a large and recent avalanche. There was no sign of the person ahead of him. Rider 1 noticed a skin track higher than normal on the slope. Most of it had been destroyed by the avalanche, but there was a small portion left.

Two skiers also approaching the area got their first view of the avalanche just before 9:30 a.m. Skier 1 called 911, reported the slide, and then raced ahead of Skier 2 to begin searching the debris. When Skier 1 arrived at the avalanche debris, Rider 1 was already searching with his transceiver below the remaining skin track. Skier 2 arrived, and the three tourers coordinated rescue efforts. They searched a large portion of the debris field and never got a transceiver signal. The team was worried about overhead hazard, and without finding a signal, they decided to discontinue their search.

The riders remained nearby and talked by phone with the 911 dispatch center, Loveland Ski Patrol, and Alpine Rescue Team. Meanwhile, the Clear Creek County Sheriff matched vehicle registrations of cars in the parking area with all people in the area. They identified one missing person and tried reaching him on his cell phone. After repeated calls went unanswered, the Sheriff's Office used the cell signal to obtain the coordinates of the phone. These were relayed to the riders at the scene. Using Google Maps on his phone, Skier 2 directed the group to the coordinates, where they saw an avalanche airbag sticking out of the snow. Rider 2 was buried on the downhill side of a few trees. Skier 1 dug out the subject's head, cleared his airway, and monitored the patient for breathing and a pulse but found neither.

Alpine Rescue Team members and Colorado Avalanche Information Center (CAIC) forecasters arrived on scene at about 12:35 p.m. They determined they could not provide additional care to Rider 2. They searched the avalanche debris with transceivers, by spot probing, and with a Recco detector, but did not find additional people in the debris.

ANALYSIS

This avalanche overran a well-used skin track and other skier tracks. Position of Rider 2 after the slide is shown. *Colorado Avalanche Information Center*

The crown face of this avalanche was up to 20 feet deep and 850 feet wide, and debris ran 500 vertical feet. The avalanche broke in a layer of faceted snow about two feet from the ground before stepping down to the ground, taking the entire season's snowpack with it. The avalanche ran into relatively flat terrain, covering tracks of riders from previous days, and it snapped numerous trees up to five inches in diameter. The slope angle of the bed surface was generally 35 degrees, but as steep as 42 degrees in places.

During the 11 days preceding this accident, the nearby Loveland Ski Area recorded 39 inches of snow, with measurable snowfall 10 out of 11 days. There were consistent westerly winds throughout this period.

The CAIC rated the backcountry avalanche danger in the Front Range zone at Considerable at all elevations on the day of the accident. A Special Avalanche Advisory (SAA) had been issued for the Front Range zone on February 12. It read, in part, "Avalanche conditions are unusual. Backcountry travelers can trigger avalanches that may break very wide and run the full length of the avalanche path. Your normal routes and safety habits may not keep you out of a dangerous avalanche."

Early snowfall in this area followed by dry weather had produced a layer of very weak depth hoar snow. Snowfall from mid-December to early January buried this weak snow layer and built a slab of stronger snow on top. Subsequent periods of dry weather allowed weak faceted snow to form on the snow surface, which was then buried by the next snowstorm or wind-loading event. This pattern repeated, and by the second week of February, the snowpack contained several weak layers of faceted snow between harder, strong slabs. All of these layers were resting on the very weak layer of depth hoar near the ground.

This avalanche ran over a well-used skin track. During unusual snowpack conditions, "normal" routes and what are considered safe spots must be re-evaluated.

Traveling alone in avalanche terrain increases the consequences if you are caught. Although this was a very large avalanche, Rider 2's head was buried only a foot beneath the snow surface. A partner that was not in the avalanche may have quickly rescued Rider 2. However, the rider did have traumatic injuries, so we don't know if a speedy recovery would have produced a different outcome.

The subject was wearing an avalanche airbag but no avalanche rescue transceiver. It is likely Rider 1 would have recovered Rider 2 much faster if the rider was wearing a transceiver. We recommend you always wear a transceiver when you are traveling in avalanche terrain, even if you are by yourself. There is always a chance another group could rescue you, and it will help search and rescue groups find you and return your remains to your family if you are killed in the mountains.

Rider 2 deployed his avalanche airbag, which may have kept him from being buried deeper, but it did not keep his head from being buried under the snow. When rescuers found Rider 2, he was wearing the sternum strap on his airbag pack but not the leg loop. The sternum strap was pushed up against his neck. As with any safety device, it is important to follow the manufacturer's instructions. Most airbags come with a leg loop to prevent the pack's sternum strap from sliding up and posing a choking hazard. It also keeps your upper body closer to the bag.

The other backcountry tourers in the area on this Sunday morning made valiant efforts. Skiers 1 and 2 and Rider 1 alerted 911 immediately and coordinated their own rescue effort before organized rescue arrived. The three tourers' actions led to the relatively quick recovery of the victim and an efficient clearing of the accident site. (*Source: Colorado Avalanche Information Center.*)

SMALL SLIDE, LONG RIDE | Inadequate Gear, Ignored Warning
New Hampshire, Mt. Washington, Tuckerman Ravine

On January 22, 2021, at 3:20 p.m., a skier was caught by an avalanche triggered by his party and carried from near the top of Left Gully almost to the floor of Tuckerman Ravine. An approximately six-inch slab of new and wind-deposited snow released from Skier 2's feet as Skier 1 made their first turn. Skier 1 was swept into and under the moving debris and lost their skis and poles. When the flow stopped, Skier 1 was buried face-down, fortunately with their head very near the surface and able to breathe, while the rest of their body was buried by two feet or more of debris.

Skier 2 located their friend, but without a shovel was unable to dig them out. Bystanders closer to the scene began to dig out Skier 1, and others, alerted by Skier 2, soon came to assist.

ANALYSIS
Just prior to the avalanche, a snow ranger suggested to the two skiers, who did not have beacons, shovels, or probes, that they ski the lower-angled slope between Right Gully and Lobster Claw or the lower section of Left Gully—if they skied anything at all. They later told snow rangers that the excitement of new snow drove them to the top of Left Gully, where the incident then unfolded. These two were very helpful to the community by honestly sharing their story with snow rangers.

There were no natural avalanches reported that day, which carried a Moderate danger rating. (The forecast did include possible human triggering of small wind slabs.) This pair was among many poorly equipped skiers or skiers traveling alone. Reading the forecast carefully, applying safe travel techniques, and carrying the proper equipment are fundamental to recreating in avalanche terrain. It is critical to acknowledge that the majority of avalanche incidents and fatalities occur on Moderate danger-rating days, where there may isolated but large avalanches *or* widespread, smaller avalanches, such as the one on this day. Both can carry real consequences.

Of interest following this event were the readings from Skier 1's GPS watch: It recorded a total vertical drop during the avalanche of 850 feet and a maximum speed of 53 mph. (*Source: Mount Washington Avalanche Center.*)

CARRIED INTO TERRAIN TRAP | 'Low' Hazard, Skiing Alone
New Hampshire, Mt. Washington, Ammonoosuc Ravine

At around 7 a.m. on Wednesday, February 3, 2021, a New Hampshire Fish and Game officer contacted the Mount Washington Avalanche Center to ask for assistance in locating the vehicle of an individual who had been reported missing the previous night. Ian Forgays, a 54-year-old male from Vermont, had texted friends on Monday, February 1, to say he planned a day of backcountry skiing on the west side of Mt. Washington, either in Ammonoosuc Ravine or Monroe Brook, prior to the start of a significant winter storm arriving that night.

Forgays' vehicle was found at the Ammonoosuc Ravine trailhead at 10 a.m. on Wednesday morning. A ground search was organized while team leaders analyzed texts and photos the subject sent to friends in order to produce a likely timeline of events; this helped focus efforts on the area surrounding Ammonoosuc Ravine. Avalanche hazard on Wednesday morning was forecast as Considerable, following High danger the previous day. Light freezing rain and snow showers were falling at higher elevations in the search area. Small teams of three or four were sent to several likely locations to begin the ground search.

By early afternoon, advanced cell phone forensics narrowed the last known point of the subject's cell phone to an area almost directly above the main drainage of the Ammonoosuc. As searchers left the hiking trail and made their way up the drainage, they found debris and some broken trees that were evidence of recent slide activity, most likely from a widespread avalanche cycle on Tuesday, one day after the subject skied the area. At 4:25 p.m., a beacon signal was acquired by a searcher with a dog and Recco receiver beneath the largest west-northwest-facing slope of the Ammonoosuc, at around 3,950 feet. Pinpoint search techniques with an avalanche transceiver located a beacon signal 3.8 meters (12 feet 6 inches) beneath the debris, which had piled up against the face of an overhanging rock buttress.

Rescuers began to dig and probe, and as more rescuers arrived and lowered the grade of the snow by more than a meter, a probe strike was finally confirmed. Eight rescuers took turns digging for an hour and 35 minutes. When they reached the subject's body, the teams extricated it from the deep hole, lowered the subject down two pitches of steep snow and ice, and then shifted to a SKED rescue litter for transport to the road. An autopsy later identified asphyxia as the cause of death.

ANALYSIS

Texts to the Forgays' friends stated that he planned to "take advantage of low avy danger and low winds up high," prior to the onset of the winter storm. By 9 a.m. on Monday, the skier had reached treeline on Mt. Monroe, and by 11 a.m. he was near the summit of Mt. Washington. He then headed for the ravine.

On the day the subject went skiing, the avalanche danger for the area was rated as Low. Conditions included a mix of snow surfaces, ranging from ice to rimed snow to firm wind slabs, all of which are commonplace in the wind-raked alpine areas and steep ravines of the Presidential Range. The layers beneath included a widespread, wind-hammered surface dubbed the "157 Layer," after the 157 mph peak wind speed on January 24 that helped create it. Above that layer was another, softer wind slab, described in the February 1 forecast as "...smooth, hollow sounding slabs (that) are easy to identify." The Bottom Line of the forecast stated, "The potential for small avalanches of wind-drifted snow remains in isolated areas at mid and upper elevations."

It is likely that Forgays triggered one of these isolated pockets and then was carried into a bowl-like depression, where the snow was stopped by an overhanging cliff that was angled upslope. The debris pile here was deep but fairly narrow, fanning out from a 10-foot strip to about 25 feet wide by 40 feet long.

The week prior to Forgays' burial had brought only four inches of snow total to the Mt. Washington summit, with relatively low wind speeds. The cold nights and some wind loading did create slabs, but they were relatively small in size. An examination of the crown of the Forgays avalanche wasn't possible, since extreme winds and new snow the following day erased all the signs. Weather factors and observations from other areas suggest a small (D1) wind slab was most likely.

A rescuer begins to probe just after a Recco and beacon search found a signal four meters beneath the snow in Ammonoosuc Ravine. The avalanche path is the narrow strip of snow in the background, between the ice on the left and the boulders on the right. *Mount Washington Avalanche Center*

Information provided by family and friends indicates that Forgays had skied Mt Washington hundreds of times. His choice to ski that day seems informed and intentional, and his past ski missions with friends reflected an enthusiasm for any sort of skiing adventure.

Accidents like this serve as a stark reminder of the role that luck can play in our backcountry endeavors. Finding a triggerable slab in mostly safe avalanche conditions is rare but not unheard of, especially due to our [local] mountains' spatially variable wind slab avalanche problem. Accurately assessing snow and terrain and avoiding trouble throughout a lifetime of playing in the mountains is a tremendous challenge for anyone, even for the most experienced.

A skiing partner might have saved Ian Forgays' life when he triggered a small wind slab, but given the terrain trap below, maybe not. Forgays was equipped with avalanche safety gear, including an avalanche transceiver, which helped rescuers and the family immensely. But it is important to remember that even the most experienced skiers with all the correct preparations and equipment risk more when skiing alone. If there are lessons to be learned from this accident, they aren't new. Skiing technical lines, in a thin snowpack above a notorious terrain trap, with no partners, even on a Low danger day, raises the stakes tremendously. (*Source: Frank Carus, lead snow ranger, Mount Washington Avalanche Center.*)

DATA TABLES

These tables include data from all accidents in the United States and Canada that are reported in this book, plus many additional accidents for which data were available. Many climbing accidents each year are not reported, and the methodology for these tables has evolved over the years. Therefore, the tables should not be viewed as precise counts of annual climbing accidents, and the data may not represent trends over time completely accurately. Readers likely will find the most value in the distribution and patterns of demographic and causal data in Tables II and III.

TABLE I: REPORTED CLIMBING ACCIDENTS*

Year	Accidents Reported		Injured		Fatalities	
	US	CA	US	CA	US	CA
1950s	33	n/a	26	n/a	10	n/a
1960s	66	8	52	7	21	3
1970s	114	18	97	10	34	8
1980s	191	29	124	26	33	8
1990	136	25	125	24	24	4
1991	169	20	147	11	18	6
1992	175	17	144	11	43	6
1993	132	27	121	17	21	1
1994	158	25	131	25	27	5
1995	168	24	134	18	37	7
1996	139	28	100	16	31	6
1997	158	35	148	24	31	13
1998	138	24	138	18	20	1
1999	123	29	91	20	17	10
2000	150	23	121	23	24	7
2001	150	22	138	14	16	2
2002	139	27	105	23	34	6
2003	118	29	105	22	18	6
2004	160	35	140	16	35	14
2005	111	19	85	14	34	7
2006	109	n/a	89	n/a	21	n/a
2007	113	n/a	95	n/a	15	n/a
2008	112	n/a	96	n/a	19	n/a
2009	126	n/a	112	n/a	23	n/a
2010	185	n/a	151	n/a	34	n/a
2011	157	n/a	109	n/a	29	n/a
2012	140	15	121	12	30	2
2013	143	11	100	5	21	4
2014	112	10	89	8	28	1

Year	Accidents Reported		Injured		Fatalities	
	US	**CA**	**US**	**CA**	**US**	**CA**
2015	173	20	111	16	37	4
2016	175	23	134	17	32	6
2017	162	24	116	19	34	2
2018	187	17	198	12	17	5
2019	202	18	148	12	31	9
2020	157	19	118	13	28	5
TOTAL	**8,364**	**1,115**	**6,945**	**829**	**1,772**	**330**

* Table I was revised in 2021. The figures presented for the 1950s, 1960s, 1970s, and 1980s are averages of the annual totals for each decade. The category "Total Persons Involved" has been eliminated. The "Total" figures are comprehensive totals from 1951 through 2020. The complete Table I from 1951 to 2019 is archived at publications.americanalpineclub.org.

TABLE II: REPORTED ACCIDENTS BY LOCATION*

Canada*	1959–2019		2020		
Geographic Districts	**Accidents**	**Deaths**	**Accidents**	**Deaths**	**Injured**
Alberta	597	159	16	4	11
British Columbia	362	135	3	1	2
Yukon & Northwest Territories	46	30	0	0	0
Ontario	43	9	0	0	0
Québec	34	10	0	0	0
Eastern Provinces & Territories	9	2	0	0	0

United States*	1951–2019		2020		
Geographic Districts	**Accidents**	**Deaths**	**Accidents**	**Deaths**	**Injured**
Alaska	666	228	3	1	3
Arizona, Nevada, Texas	146	26	2	1	1
Northeast	1285	167	18	4	12
Southeast	290	46	15	0	14
California	1673	352	27	2	21
Central	149	19	2	0	2
Colorado	1066	264	31	8	20
Montana, Idaho, South Dakota	114	45	7	1	7
Oregon	298	134	12	3	9
Utah, New Mex.	264	78	15	2	10
Washington	2079	355	17	4	13
Wyoming	679	166	8	2	6

* The Canada section of Table II was revised in 2021. Eastern Provinces and Territories includes Nunavut, Newfoundland, and the Maritimes. In the U.S., Northeast includes New England and the Mid-Atlantic states (southward to Maryland/Delaware), plus Ohio and Indiana. Southeast includes West Virginia, Virginia, Kentucky, and states farther south. Central incudes Michigan and the Upper Midwest (minus South Dakota), plus Missouri and Arkansas.

TABLE III: ACCIDENT CHARACTERISTICS AND CAUSES

	1951–2019 USA	1959–2019 CAN*	2020 USA	2020 CAN
Terrain				
Rock	5765	618	120	15
Snow	2813	386	25	2
Ice	326	31	8	1
Water	26	3	0	0
Unknown	26	11	4	1
Ascent or Descent				
Ascent	4554	662	96	13
Descent	1608	422	41	4
Unknown	386	19	14	0
Other[1]	59	6	6	2
Climbing Style[†]				
Alpine/Mountaineering	62	3	46	10
Ice and mixed climbing	1	3	5	0
Traditional rock climbing	71	3	49	4
Sport climbing	28	2	28	3
Big-wall climbing	3	0	1	0
Bouldering	6	1	4	0
Top-rope	4	0	1	0
Free solo or DWS	5	2	4	0
Ski mountaineering	7	0	5	1
Other/Not Applicable/Unknown	12	0	14	1
Rope Position[†]				
Leading	50	3	56	7
Seconding	5	0	2	0
Top-roping	1	0	1	0
Roped but not belayed	4	0	2	0
Unroped	33	2	39	5
Rappelling	20	2	12	0
Lowering	9	0	6	0
Belaying	3	2	7	1
Other/Not Applicable/Unknown	52	7	32	6

[†] "Climbing style" and "rope position" categories were introduced in 2021. (The first two columns for each category include data from 2019.) "Rope position" tabulates the position or activity of the person(s) most directly affected by an accident (injured or killed, stranded, near miss, etc.), at the time the incident occurred. "Roped but not belayed" includes simul-climbing and glacier travel. "Unroped" includes bouldering.

	1951–2019 USA	1959–2019 CAN*	2020 USA	2020 CAN
Immediate Causes**				
Fall on rock	4374	333	66	10
Fall on ice (formerly snow or ice)	1252	227	5	1
Fall on snow	22	0	11	1
Falling rock, ice, object	737	1	10	2
Illness	615	0	3	0
Stranded / Lost	472	0	9	2
Avalanche	465	0	5	0
Rappel Failure/Error[3]	341	0	5	0
Lowering Error[6]	457	0	7	0
Fall from anchor	2	0	1	0
Anchor failure	4	1	7	0
Exposure	291	0	0	0
Glissade error	249	0	0	0
Protection pulled out	393	0	1	0
Failure to follow route	262	0	0	0
Fall into crevasse/moat	198	0	2	1
Faulty use of crampons	128	0	0	0
Ascending too fast	88	0	0	0
Skiing[4]	91	0	2	0
Lightning	69	0	0	0
Equipment failure	19	0	0	0
Other[5]	647	1	6	1
Unknown	117	0	3	1
Contributing Causes***				
Climbing unroped	1134	178	14	1
Inexperience	1121	209	7	2
Placed no/inadequate protection	966	115	0	0
Inadequate equipment/clothing	794	78	6	1
Weather	556	84	1	0
Climbing alone	482	74	4	1
No helmet	416	77	2	0
Inadequate belay	331	30	4	1
Protection pulled out (climber placed)	17	1	17	1
Protection pulled out (fixed)	3	0	1	0
Inadequate knot	4	0	2	0
Inadequate backup	11	0	5	0
Rope too short	n/a	n/a	3	0

	1951–2019 USA	1959–2019 CAN*	2020 USA	2020 CAN
Poor position	276	36	6	1
Darkness	195	23	0	0
Party separated	146	12	2	0
Loose rock/failure to test holds	153	54	12	3
Off-route	150	20	9	2
Failure to self-arrest	7	0	5	0
Exposure	70	16	0	0
Illness	49	10	0	0
Equipment failure	28	8	0	0
Other	354	104	11	2
Age of Individuals				
Under 15	1253	12	2	0
15-20	1375	206	6	0
21-25	1703	263	22	1
26-30	1621	221	23	2
31-35	2232	23	23	0
36-50	3631	150	21	2
Over 50	496	39	14	1
Unknown	2495	628	57	15
Sex[6]				
Male	672	80	115	9
Female	193	17	43	3
Not known	150	18	11	10
Experience Level				
Novice	2018	309	8	2
Intermediate	1907	367	12	0
Expert	2700	521	65	10
Unknown	2941	631	80	10
Month				
January	284	28	3	0
February	271	63	8	0
March	417	82	9	0
April	526	46	8	0
May	1108	72	14	3
June	1382	86	22	3
July	2196	280	17	4
August	1273	215	26	5
September	2121	84	16	3

	1951–2019 USA	1959–2019 CAN*	2020 USA	2020 CAN
October	570	44	19	0
November	280	25	10	0
December	146	28	4	1
Unknown	108	3	1	0

Type of Injury/Illness (Data since 1984. Fracture and internal injury breakouts introduced in 2020.)

	1951–2019 USA	1959–2019 CAN*	2020 USA	2020 CAN
Fracture: lower extremity	33	2	39	7
Fracture: upper extremity	12	3	4	1
Fracture: other	23	1	16	1
Spine injury/fracture	15	1	13	2
Total Fractures	1912	268	72	11
Laceration	919	90	13	1
Abrasion	476	80	9	0
Bruise	645	91	12	0
Sprain/Strain	515	38	4	0
Head Injury/TBI	434	40	27	1
Internal: chest	5	0	4	0
Internal: abdomen	0	0	2	0
Hypothermia	190	20	2	0
Frostbite	167	13	1	0
Dislocation	193	17	1	0
Puncture	67	14	3	0
Acute mountain sickness	57	0	0	0
HAPE	101	1	0	0
HACE	41	1	0	0
Other[7]	513	65	9	1
None	443	207	13	2

N.B. 1986 and 1997 editions included some repeated data from prior years. Corrections are reflected in cumulative data.

* No Canada data from 2006–2011; includes new data from 2012–2020

** "Fall on snow" and "anchor failure" are new in 2021; past years combined falls on snow and ice. "Protection pulled out" combines two former categories; in this section, the protection pulling out must directly cause the fall.

*** Categories introduced in 2021 include "Protection pulled out (climber placed)" and "Protection pulled out (fixed)"; these replace "Nut/cam pulled out" and "Piton/ice screw pulled out." Other new categories in 2021 are "Inadequate knot," "Inadequate backup," "Rope too short," and "Failure to self-arrest."

1   Some reported accidents happen when climbers are at the top or bottom of a route, during an approach, or (rarely) in camp. This category was created in 2001. The category "unknown" is primarily because of solo climbers.

2   These are illnesses/injuries that led directly or indirectly to an accident or rescue, such as HAPE.

3   These include uneven ropes, pendulum swings, attaching device incorrectly, and stuck ropes. Prior years' data included some lowering errors, anchor failures, and inadequate backups (now their own categories).

4   This category covers ski mountaineering. Backcountry ski touring or snowshoeing incidents, including those involving avalanches, are not counted in these tables.

5   These included falls during approaches (2), leg stuck in crack (2), snakebite, stranded by avalanche danger, rockfall destroying anchor (2), running in crampons, dropped crampon, collapsed ice curtain, and others in 2020.

6   Categories introduced in 2016. Lowering errors include rope too short, miscommunication, and no knot in rope end.

7   These included dehydration, rope burn, various shoulder and knee injuries, snakebite, heat stroke, amputated finger, and others in 2020. Note: Injuries are counted only once in each category for a given incident. For example, an accident that results in two broken ankles will only be listed once under "Fracture: lower extremity."

MOUNTAIN RESCUE ASSOCIATION

We Never Charge for Rescue

CLIMBERS HELPING CLIMBERS SINCE 1959.

MRA member Rocky Mountain Rescue Group in action at Eldorado Canyon, Colorado. Photo by Alison Sheets.

Courage. Commitment. Compassion.

www.mra.org